CW00551935

Thanks to:
Tamika Abaka-Wood for working tirelessly to make sure every last detail has been covered and that this whole thing could actually happen.

David Burton, our illustrator, for the beautiful sketch notes that make sense of the games and stories.

Ali Augur, our designer, for giving us structure and rules that turn the pages of scribbles and script into an actual book.

D&AD for hosting us during Judging Week 2015 and treating us like part of their team.

All of our contributors for taking the time out of their busy lives to come and talk, share and play.

And lastly, to all our merry band of proof-readers who responded via Twitter, LinkedIn, Facebook and Instagram, to help save what you're reading from being gobbledygook.

Photography credits: Ash Narod, Michael A. Sheehan, Aubrey Johnson, Paul Winch-Furness, Justin Sutcliffe, Hugo Glendinning, Dave Morgan, Helen Maybanks, Abhijit Bhatlekar.

ISBN: 978-0-9932883-0-2

Printed in the United Kingdom.

Ben & Andrew's Bumper book of fun and Games

A compendium of creative tools
for better problem solving

Ben&Andrew's bumper book of fun
and games - a compendium of creative
tools for better problem solving.

Written by Andrew Missingham
Edited by Ben Gallagher
Illustrated by David Burton
Design & Art Direction by Ali Augur
Project Management by Tamika Abaka-Wood
Foreword by Mark Earls

Featuring creative insights by Richard Alston CBE,
Felix Barrett, James Bowthorpe, Vaibhav Chhabra,
Melanie Chisholm, Robert Cohan CBE, Charlie Dark,
Sonia Dove, Scott Graham, Kwame Kwaten, Maria McCloy,
Amelia-Belle Missingham, Martin Morales, Shailesh Prabhu,
Lord Puttnam, Katherine Ryan, Nitin Sawhney and
Dylan Williams.

Made in 5 days at D&AD Judging Week 2015.

d.i.y. contents

Fill this in with stuff you want to easily return to...

	page

FOREWORD
MARK EARLS

In one of his very last interviews, the late great Kurt Vonnegut was asked if he had any advice for the young people who had so taken his novels to heart. Yes, he replied. "Join a gang - any gang. Just join a gang".

Not, you understand, because he recommended a life of dissolution, petty or violent crime and internecine warfare, but rather being the wise old anthropologist that he was, he recognised that our lives are best lived out in the company of the right others. Yes, we need others for safety and security and all the obvious stuff, but also because embracing the right social context - the right gang - allows us to become ourselves more fully. To explore our talents and our abilities and harness those of our peers and compatriots.

This is the imperative behind this fabulous book: it says "here is our gang. Here is what we believe, about creativity and about strategy and about business. Here is what we do, together with our collaborators and workmates. Join us!"

It is in effect a highly entertaining recruitment ad which reveals itself by layers: both in its subject matter, in the interviews and experiences which it reflects upon so playfully; and in the manner of its construction over five days, rather than (as I know to my own cost) over many months that such a book normally takes to write.

And in doing so, this book embodies a new way of thinking about strategy and creativity - it shows these two not as different things, not as oil and water, not even not as sequential things, but two sides of the same coin which spin happily together.

And they are both about doing rather than merely talking and theorising. About play and playfulness. About enjoying your work.

It's a high-wire act that Ben&Andrew pull off effortlessly, just as you'd expect if you've ever worked with them before. It's playful to its bones - as they are and we all need to be if we want to solve the problems in front of us; it feels natural, rather than forced or over-thought; it creates its own irresistible beat.

So if what it says to you feels like the kind of thing you'd like to be doing - as a colleague or a client then maybe you've found your kind of gang here.

Kurt has one more thing to add here: in one of his letters to the novelist Mary Bancroft, he observes that "most people don't have good gangs, so they are doomed to cowardice.... The utopian dreaming I do now has to do with encouraging cheerfulness and bravery for everyone by the formation of good gangs".

Ben&Andrew's seems like a good gang to me. And there are precious few of those around, let me tell you.

Mark Earls, London 2015.

INTRODUCTION

Hello and welcome to Ben&Andrew's bumper book of fun and games. We want this book to be a tool that you can use to solve your problems by using our methods and the creative insights from our friends and collaborators. So whether you're growing a business, you're working towards global change, or you're creating world-class cultural content, we've made this book for you.

Our plan was to write this book in five days.

Yep. Five.

The thing is, we had the book planned for about a year. It sat in the "important, but not urgent" box for all that time. To get it done, we had to make it both urgent AND important. So we talked to our friends at D&AD and asked if we could write it live at their Awards Judging Week. They said yes.

gulp!

That lit a fire under us and provided the urgency we needed. Dates to work with. A place to be. Lots of witnesses to hold us to account and a clock ticking a crescendo.

Like the work we co-create with our clients, we knew we couldn't do it on our own, so we rounded up the nicest and smartest people we knew to make the book with us. In our team, we were lucky enough to have the best creative brains in the business - the likes of Punchdrunk's Felix Barrett, film legend Lord David Puttnam, musician Nitin Sawhney, award winning hairstylist Sonya Dove and DJ-turned-restaurateur Martin Morales. Our oldest contributor was 90. Our youngest, six and a half.

The promise we gave ourselves was to publish whatever we had written in five days. And so here it is. What you're holding (aside from the disposal of a dungheap of typographic errors) is the book that we sent to the printer at 6pm on day five and were proof-reading by 7.15pm the same evening.

This book is still unfinished. It'll only be complete when you've contributed to it and started playing with it yourself - that's why we've left space for you to add notes and create new games of your own. We'd love to hear how you get on, and we very much hope our little book proves as enjoyable, inspiring and just plain useful to you, as putting it together has done for us.

on why strategy doesn't work (and what to do instead)

Hey, maybe we need a STRATEGY!

When it comes to deciding what work we do, we aim to balance the need to sustain a business with working with people and projects that appeal to our hearts. This means that even in a short time we've been lucky enough to do a really exciting variety of projects for a diverse group of clients, from Punchdrunk and Frantic Assembly, to Microsoft and Wella, to Unicef and RockCorps. But there's a flip side. To those who haven't worked with us yet, we've spent a lot of time answering the question:

"What exactly is it that you do?"

We've proudly defied categorisation (we're particularly fond of the phrase "the thing you're most likely to find in a pigeonhole is pigeon shit") but having a broad spectrum of projects, clients and categories that we work in can make it difficult for others to frame you, explain your value to others, pass work your way and (ultimately) attribute a budget line to you.

When clients think of us at all, their most obvious starting point is that we are a strategy company. But the problem we have is that strategy hardly ever sticks. It's mostly written in isolation from the client, their world and real problems. It's often presented once and then quickly forgotten, lost amongst a pile of papers. So the question is, if we don't do strategy, what do we do ?

Over coffee a little while ago Andrew's friend Feargal Sharkey said that he thought what we did was 'provocative strategy'. This was really helpful. If we want strategy to stick, often it's better to explore, notice dissonance or challenge an opportunity and then share this with the client, provoking them to think anew, rather than present them a final conclusion and hope they like it. Provocation can be used as the key that unlocks strategy. If what you've noticed is founded in reality, the client will often look for directed activity (strategy) that responds to the challenges your provocation uncovers. This is then best co-created with the client.

So our process doesn't go: research, insight then strategy. It goes research, insight, provocation and then co-creation (of the strategy)

With this direction of travel, and provocation as our central focus we find more interesting answers and gather more interesting responses. Our clients and their people are more likely to ask questions, explore what our provocation means to their businesses, then look to co-create strategy with us. We have found that this co-created strategy is more likely to stick.

So where does this place us?

We think that we sit at an intersection. It's between a creative agency (who generate and produce brilliant ideas but often doesn't have the business influence to affect the entire client's business) and a management consultancy (who is called in to change the shape or direction of a business but doesn't have the creative skills or approaches to unlock new and unexpected ways of doing things).

We believe there is a need for a company with this combination of skills and breadth of focus because for too long clients have been paying others to claw through their pigeon shit.

Provocation is at the heart of everything we do, so this book is built around it. We came up with eleven provocations that we have a hunch might be where to look if you want a better, more creative business (or you want to be a more creative individual). In eleven chapters, the book explores each provocation in turn, through interviews, stories and games, with a space for you to add thoughts, stories and games of your own (after all, if we're co-creating, you're along for the ride too, aren't you?)

But before we get to the provocations, and because they're a key way we play, let's ask two experts: what is a game?

AMELIA-BELLE MISSINGHAM

Amelia-Belle is six and a half years old. Her favourite things are drawing (you can see a portfolio of her drawings on her Tumblr site: a-b-sees.tumblr.com) music, cooking, reading and playing games. She's an expert at playing games. Her favourite game is "It" (the UK name for "Tag").

AB: [reading two cards]: "Amelia-Belle Missingham. What is a game?"

B&A: What do you think a game is, Amelia-Belle?

AB: A game is something you play, like imagine I was with my wooden horsey, a game is something you play with it. A game should be fun.

B&A: Can you play a game on your own, or does it have to be with other people?

AB: You can play on your own, but if there's a person available, then you can include them in the game.

B&A: Is it best to play games on your own or with other people?

AB: It's best to play games with other people.

B&A: Why is that best?

AB: Imagine I was playing "Snap" and I had to play it on my own, then there would be no one else to win.

7

B&A. Does having someone else who can win make playing a game more fun?

AB: Yes, because if I was doing my game with my little [imaginary] sister Lucy, then she'd just get in the way and would have to sit in bed and have to play with her toys, but if you and Mummy helped to play Snap, and you won, Dada, it would be much more fun.

B&A: So "Snap" is a game you can play with cards. What other kinds of games are there?

AB: You can play "Nature" [AB fetches four character toys from her nature table], with my Mother Mouse and my three little ones.

B&A: And what kind of game would you invent with those guys?

[AB furtively looks under the skirt of one of the little guys]

AB: "Bum bum! [AB and Daddy giggle].

AB: I would get out my little wooden horse and I'd take them for a ride.

B&A: So is the game about pretending they're real?

AB: Yes, and the littlest of the little guys is called "Snowdrop."

B&A: And do all games pretend things are real?

AB: No, "it" is where you try to catch someone and it doesn't include toys.

B&A: And while you were talking you lined Mother Mouse and the three little guys on the wooden horse so nicely. Where are they going to go now?

AB: They're going to go to Fruit Peanut Butter Toast Land. And I'm going to feed Mother Mouse a strawberry [AB brings a strawberry up to Mother Mouse's mouth.]

B&A: So, other than playing with other people, what is it that makes a game fun?

AB: You can make a game fun by using some explanation and using toys. So if I was to take this bird

8

[picks up small wooden bird toy] and leaned it a bit down and forward, it would look like it was sad. But mostly, to make a game not fun, is to have someone not to play with.

B&A: You know you said that in playing the game the bird was sad…?

[AB changes the position of the bird so it is no longer looking down and forward] And now it's happy!

[Daddy laughs]

B&A: Yes, now it's looking up, it's happy! But is the bird in real life, or is it pretend?

AB: It's pretend because the bird doesn't talk or move or fly.

B&A: So it's a pretend bird, right? But in the game, do you imagine that the bird is real, or do you know even in the game that the bird is pretend?

AB: I know that it's not real.

B&A: What are rules for in games?

AB: If I was playing "Hide & Seek", you have to play by the rules, otherwise you'd know where people are hiding.

B&A: So do the rules make the game better or worse?

AB: The rules make the game better. Daddy, go and hide! [Daddy does what he's asked and gets up and hides in the porch of the house]. Okay. So now you're hiding, Daddy, but I'm peeking so I know where you're hiding. And now I run and I open the door where you're hiding and I say "found you!"

B&A: And does knowing where Daddy is hiding, because you're peeking make the game better or worse?

AB: Worse, because I came straight to where he was hiding. The thing that's good that's not knowing is… Daddy, you close your eyes and I'll hide this time [AB goes and hides].

B&A: Daddy is really closing his eyes now, Amelia-Belle.

AB: Now come and find me [Daddy goes looking for AB]

B&A: I'm trying to work out what's making this feeling of not-knowing feel good, AB. How would you describe that feeling? What would you call it?

AB: I'd call that feeling a feeling of mystery. It's a mystery for everyone who is playing: the looker, because they don't know where the hider is hiding, and for the hider, because they don't know when the looker will find them.

B&A: Tell me about the boy we met in Santa Monica who was too young and spoiled the game we played.

AB: What was his name again?

B&A: I can't remember, darling, but he was with Sachi and Lauren.

AB: No it was Laura, daddy.

B&A: Oh yes, Laura.

AB: He kept peeking and he kept knowing where I hid the truck. It spoiled the game because I wanted them to not know where I was hiding the truck.

B&A: Do you think it spoiled the game just for you, or for Sachi and Laura too?

AB: For Sachi and Laura too, because then they don't get to look properly.

B&A: That's all my questions. Do you have any questions for me?

Wait. [AB goes to her drawing table and after around a minute comes back with two pieces of paper with writing on, like Daddy had given her].

AB: This is going to be a tricky one

[Daddy reads] "Daddy. What is a life?"

SHAILESH PRABHU

Shailesh is a game designer from Mumbai, India. He founded Yellow Monkey Studios seven years ago and has since received numerous game design and entrepreneurship awards from all over the globe. He is an advisor to NASSCOM Game Developer Conference and a consultant at Casual Connect Conference, which aims to enable Indian talent to be showcased in Western markets. In his spare time, he also mentors aspiring developers. With his company, Yellow Monkey, he has created "HUEBRIX" and "It's Just a Thought" amongst other critically and commercially successful games.

B&A: Where do you think great innovation comes from, Shailesh?

SP: I think that the best innovation lives where you least expect. This is a bit of a mantra at Yellow Monkey, my games company. Whenever we talk to people about games they have a picture of art and design. But we don't have an artist or a designer. We have a technical team. When they hear this they are really surprised - it breaks the expectation of where game design can come from. They expect there to be an artist because they are used to big complex, triple A games (like Grand Theft Auto). In India, they aren't aware of more simple digital games - that are still great games but just aren't as sexy. In our opinion to make a great game you don't need to be flashy. For example look at MineCraft - it's a low-res texture on square blocks. It succeeded as a game because it was so much fun and had great gameplay. The unexpected outcome was it made the look a defining style for games.

The other provocation I like is 'the more I know, the more I know I know fuck all'. This is interesting because, in my experience, the more you know, normally the more you become set in your ways. It's so hard for people to un-learn something and learn something new to replace it. Un-learning is such an important skill that very few people can do. Sometimes you are so bound by what you know, that you can't think beyond this existing view. So, it's not about forgetting something, it's about breaking out of existing behaviours.

B&A: Why are games your passion, Shailesh? Why have you chosen to make a career of making games?

SP: I've been playing games since I was a boy of eight. I really enjoy them. When I was a kid they gave me this whole world that has nothing to do with the real world but it has its own rules and systems. When I realised I could make these worlds and get paid for it I was in! Games are a creative medium that have audio, visual and interaction as a way to deliver an experience and the tiniest adjustment in the nature of the interaction can alter the meaning you are delivering - that's really exciting to me.

B&A: What does it take to make a worthwhile game?

SP: I think you need to be able to distill what fun is. You have to figure out where the fun lies in the game and then when you have done this you can deliver it in any medium. To find the fun you have to make prototypes and test them on people. You don't talk to the people you're testing with, you just watch and observe. You really want to talk to them but you have to hold back, and see where they react and engage. You keep doing this until you get clear on whether there is fun and where it is. The reason we don't talk to them is because it brings baggage. It's true that by not asking, you don't know why people are doing certain things, but if you ask them and engage directly, then they will most often give you an answer that they think they think. The truth is, though, they don't know for sure either! So it's best to watch how they react and work from that.

B&A: Do you make games with a person in mind? Or are they for anybody?

SP: We don't have a specific audience. We make games for lots of different kinds of people but ultimately we make games that we like. We then find an audience that we think will enjoy what we have created. Kids are always really fun to make games for because they are good at playing them. Their lack of experience of many game formats mean they don't have such an ingrained preference around the kind of games they enjoy. They are also really quick to learn. The fastest person to complete our last game was five years old. He didn't even have to think about it.

11 PROVOCATIONS

1. Listening takes all five senses

2. The more I know the more I know I know fuck all

3. There's a world outside your manor and I want you to see it

4. Be the person everyone wants on the tour bus

5. Have a Californian optimism and a wry British sense of humour

6. The work you do best is the work you love is the work you do best

7. When in doubt choose

8. The further the thesis from the antithesis the greater the synthesis

9. More does not equal better

10. There's a best before date on every right answer

11. We are not storytellers we are set builders

1. LISTENING TAKES ALL FIVE SENSES

Listening is hard. You can dedicate your life to it, and still not be great. We've learned that a key to getting better is to listen with all five senses.

When it comes to listening to what's going on around you, often the answer's not received through your ears. Being sensitive to how something looks, feels, tastes and even smells can give you more useful feedback that can give you a much better sense of what's going on. Often this can be cultural. For instance, working in Rwanda, people say it's not if someone says yes to you, but how. In another example, we know of a UK government-funded project that was independently reviewed and given a clean bill of health (and subsequent funding), where the reviewer was totally blind-sided because while everything looked good on the surface, he couldn't recognise the tell-tale smell of crack cocaine on the premises which pointed to the venue's deep dysfunction. The place closed its doors within two years, mired in scandal and acrimony.

As well as allowing us to learn better, listening with all five senses gives us ways to create answers that suit different learning styles. An all-sensory approach can lead to solutions that play to the five ways that people tend to interact and learn from the world, be they primarily visual, auditory, kinesthetic, olfactory or even gustatory.

But most of all, listening for us isn't an individual pursuit, it's a team sport. As well as involving all senses, it needs to be seen from a variety of perspectives. To see from these perspectives, we have to realise that getting people to be honest is the start, but it's just the first step to discovering a truth that can point to your problem's answer.

Back in the 80's there was a great advertisement for the Guardian newspaper (by BMP's John Webster). It showed a young frightened-looking skinhead running away as an apparently pursuing car rounded a corner. Accompanied by a voiceover, the scene ran again, but this time seen from a different vantage point. The second view showed a frightening looking skinhead running towards a frightened looking businessman, who clutches a briefcase close to his chest by way of defence. One last time the scene is played. The third time you see the falling bricks from a building site above, that the skinhead is pushing the man to be saved from being hit by. Each is an honest view of the world. Only the complete view comes close to capturing anything like the truth.

This chapter gives some ideas on how to get better at the vital skill of listening, in order to get honest perspectives, so you can uncover collective truths. Armed with these accumulated truths you can arrive at an understanding of collective, cultural behaviour, which can lead to the diagnosis of underlying issues and problems so you can then best solve them.

LORD
PUTTNAM

Lord Puttnam is one of the UK's most respected and celebrated film producers and educators. He was awarded a CBE in 1992, a knighthood in 1995, and was then appointed to the House of Lords in 1997. He spent 30 years as an independent film producer and won 10 Oscars, 25 Baftas and the Palme D'Or at Cannes. He now works extensively in public policy related to education, the environment, and the 'creative and communications' industries. Through this work he founded the National Teaching Awards and he was also president of UNICEF UK. He has served as a trustee of the Tate Gallery and the Science Museum amongst many other organisations.

DP: I'm not as good at listening as I'd like to be. Listening is harder than talking, particularly when you find yourself (whether you like it or not) preparing the next thing you want to say when you're going through the motions of listening to what someone else is saying. I think the notion of listening and absorbing, and not worrying about your next response, reaction or point you want to get across actually requires a fair amount of self-discipline.

B&A: How do you balance that reflection with also needing to answer back?

DP: To an extent sometimes it balances itself, depending on the information you want to gather from the person you're with. I am a compulsive note-taker. If I am in 'note-taking mode', I am very much in a listening mode. There are other times, when I also have things I want to say and in order to have a civilised conversation you try and create a 70/30 situation with the person you're with. Focusing on the 30 that they can offer is quite difficult when there's 100% you want to give to the conversation. I think it is the difference between 'listening' and 'really listening': you can appear to listen but are you prepared to absorb what that other person is trying to say, and what they're saying isn't simply the pause between what you want to say.

B&A: Do you think that's always been the case, or has that been something that has changed over time?

DP: My instinct is that people are less good at listening now than they used to be. One of the reasons for that is that listening became something you got quite good at with the radio. As a young lad, I didn't have a TV set until I was 13 so radio was our connection with the outside world. I spent a lot of time listening to the radio. It was a big factor in our lives and had the ability to surprise you because you never knew what was coming next and didn't have another channel to flip to. So without knowing it you were probably training yourself to be a better listener. Today, if you're not hearing what you want to hear then you tend to flip channels or do something else. What happens is information becomes a series of reaffirmations of what you already think rather than the ability to open yourself up to something you'd never even considered before.

B&A: Do you think you can tell if someone is really listening?

DP: I'd like to think I can but I'm not certain. Tell-tale signs are when people start answering a question before you've asked it and the answer is not what you were going to ask about.

B&A: Do you think you can you teach yourself how to listen?

DP: Probably, but only I think if you've discovered the real value that you learn from the experience when you really listened. I don't think you can learn to listen in a school setting, because it is forced. You can learn to listen if you are continually involved in things that fascinate you with people who fascinate you. I was very lucky, I had a Dad who was in the news business, and what he happened to say when I saw him at weekends, I thought was endlessly interesting, so I did learn to listen to my Dad.

B&A: What is the best advice you've never taken?

DP: Slow down! People are still saying that to me now. It probably would have been good advice, but at the same time it wouldn't have worked for me. I don't really have the choice: I am very driven and I am goal-orientated. These goals are what have made life a lot richer for me. It is getting things done. It is also a weakness though, if someone has a problem I find it much easier to try and find a solution, as opposed to just being sympathetic. I like to solve problems, I don't have that innate empathetic quality.

B&A: If you are a 'doing' person, and are doing things quickly, do you tend to make more mistakes?

DP: Probably. But you can't avoid making mistakes. The thing is, smart people avoiding making the same mistake more than once. I've never had a problem with making mistakes. I am self-critical of my own work. I, almost in a quite brutal way, pull it apart and take a look at what went wrong. I could go through all of my 30 movies and of the 20 that are not crappy, I could tell you all of the things that I would change today. It's not surprising I find it quite difficult to watch my own films!

B&A: Does that mean you're actually not happy with the work you've done?

DP: No, that's the wrong word. I am kind of dissatisfied and irritated. What upsets you is when you know you made a decision as a compromise for what were quite good reasons at the time. I once failed to fully understand the importance of a casting decision of a small part of a movie, it hurt the film and I to this day believe it could have won an Oscar if it wasn't for this decision.

B&A: Who do you think is a particularly good listener?

DP: Robert Bolt was a good listener. It was partly because he had a stroke and therefore it took him a while to answer. There was a natural pause between anything you said and the time he answered. He had to think about and synthesise his answer to you. I think that is quite important.

If I had a disability that only allowed me to answer in 15-20 words I'd choose those words quite carefully. One of the things I miss is dictating letters, because the physical process requires that you turn over in your mind what you're saying, in terms of thoughts, sentences and paragraphs. It is really really a skill that challenges you.

The most impressive listeners I have ever dealt with are special needs teachers. They are brilliant listeners because they're listening for a response which is very often not oral so they are constantly waiting and have to be very patient. They work in tiny incremental changes so they'll get a kid to move a thing from 'there' to 'there' and it takes them all day. What is so impressive is that these minimal victories are absorbed into their own lives. They see the world in terms of very small but incremental improvements, and it makes them far more satisfied. The things they are out for are often not noticed by anyone else. They're not looking for visible successes, but small internal changes.

Every single person living would be significantly improved as a listener if they spent a year as a special needs teacher: I'd go that far.

B&A: Which world do you think is more honest: advertising, politics or film making?

DP: Film making, without any shadow of doubt, because films are going to be around for a long time. You really can't afford, if you've got any pride at all, for any part of your movie to become deeply challengeable. Politicians skip from day to day, advertising has constant self-justification to itself which is really about serving the needs of its clients whether it likes to admit it or not. Politicians believe themselves to be answerable to their colleagues in their party, rather than to society. Film makers are answerable to the audience, and the audience represents society.

B&A: And films will be around forever...

DP: So if you fuck up you've got to live with it for a long long time.

SONYA DOVE

Born in England, Sonya Dove is owner of The Doves Hair Salon in Santa Monica, California. Along with Christopher Dove, with whom she co-founded her studio, she has won numerous awards including Hair Color USA's "Hair Colorist of the Year" and "Most Inspiring Hair Colorists." They were the first recipients of the North American Hairstylist Association's "Masters Hairstylists of the Year" and received the USA National Cosmetology Association's "Icons of the Year". Sonya is the US ambassador for Wella's Global Trend Vision, and creative director for Intercoiffure's Hair Colour Council.

B&A: What is creativity to you, Sonya?

SD: Creativity is about making someone else feel good. It's about inspiring them. People come into my salon in all sorts of moods. For me, being able to change their mood and make them more positive, with something as personal as their hair, is a real gift. You can feel their energy lift when you cut and colour someone's hair.

B&A: And where do you look for inspiration?

SD: It's more "how" than "where". The thing is you have to really look hard - like when you study the subtle colours in the rocks of Lake Powell. Once you've looked (and you can see), it's up to you to make connections. For instance, I love the wings of butterflies - not just their patterns and vivid colours, but also the ways the colours are made more distinct. If you look closely, you see that most patterns on butterflies are separated by black lines. These work to make the colours stand out. I started connecting this with other places where I saw the same effect - everywhere from bubble graffiti writing to ancient stained glass windows. As a colourist for hair, I'm interested in how to create new designs that are not only distinctive, but really stand out, so I started experimenting with this "bordered" effect on hair.

B&A: I want to go back to the start, to the (forgive the pun) roots of your creativity. What were you like at school?

SD: Honestly, I hated school. I was useless and left with practically no 'O' Levels at all. The one thing I got was an A grade in art. With art, I understood it. But the failure in school made me rebel. I didn't see the point, so I actively looked for something else. After school I did a secretarial course, just so I could get working, but pretty soon after that the parents of my then boyfriend (who became my husband and business partner for 27 years) told both of us that we should enrol in a local hair and beauty course. I never looked back. We opened a little two-seater salon in Paignton in the west of England, started developing our craft, putting in for awards, started winning them, then grew from there.

B&A: So to be a great hairdresser, is it all about the craft?

SD: No, for me the craft is a given. For me, the most important thing is to be a great listener. You have to let the client talk and take in every bit of information. You have to listen with all your senses. To an extent this can be taught, but there has to be a "seed" there, that you allow to blossom. This isn't a mechanical process, it's passionate. Being a good listener also means that you have to give yourself over and leave all your rubbish at home. You have to shut off the talk in your head and be totally present. If you're down, a client can sense it in a moment. I've had to send stylists home because their heads weren't right. So it's a performance to an extent, but not from the brain, from the heart.

B&A: I've heard that from a lot of the Wella stylists and colourists I've worked with - that 'heart-centred' approach. Why is hair such an emotional business?

SD: When you change your hair, you're putting your reflection in someone else's hands. That's incredibly personal. For me, to be a hairdresser you have to embrace this spirituality. You have to have raw, open honesty and total integrity.

snap

ENCOURAGES HONESTY & INDIVIDUAL POINTS OF VIEW
+ HELPS YOU SPOT INCONSISTENCIES & PATTERNS OF OPINION

"SNAP!"

1. It's a simple game that you probably played as a kid ....
SET A QUESTION on an area of enquiry, like "WHAT ARE YOUR VALUES?"

2. EVERYONE GETS **5** CARDS & writes down their own answers

(USE A THICK PEN to KEEP IT SHORT)

3. Integrity — SNAP! SNAP! SNAP!
CARDS ARE READ OUT & "SNAP!" called for any matches

4. REVIEW the cards, & how they are grouped ....

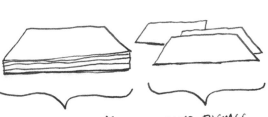

IMMEDIATE SNAPS
Recognise consistency & show where the ENERGY lies

CLOSE THEMES
Help open up. great discussion

'LONERS'
Prove interesting for conversation & often form the EDGES of OPINION

23

OUR GAME HERE ⬆

24

dominoes

A GREAT GAME for UNDERSTANDING an ORGANISATION'S CULTURE

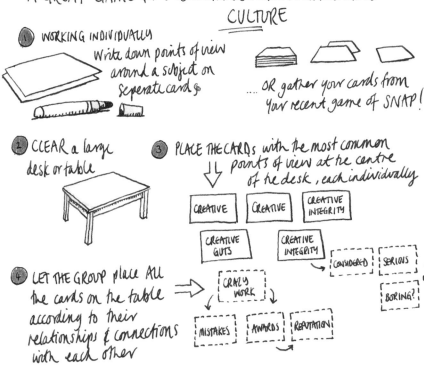

① WORKING INDIVIDUALLY
Write down points of view around a subject on seperate cards

.... OR gather your cards from your recent game of SNAP!

② CLEAR a large desk or table

③ PLACE THE CARDs with the most common points of view at the centre of the desk, each individually

CREATIVE   CREATIVE   CREATIVE INTEGRITY

CREATIVE GUTS   CREATIVE INTEGRITY

CONSIDERED   SERIOUS

④ LET THE GROUP place ALL the cards on the table according to their relationships & connections with each other

CRAZY WORK

BORING!

MISTAKES   AWARDS   REPUTATION

⑤ ALLOW THE GROUP to work alone, & notice not just where they place the cards, but WHY they place them there, and how they work together as a group

⑥ ASK the group to SHARE what they have just created

YOUR GAME HERE

NOTES:

2. THE MORE I KNOW THE MORE I KNOW I KNOW FUCK ALL

The oft-touted expression in government and education circles "life long learning" has always seemed a bit of a tautology. If you're not learning, are you really alive at all, in any meaningful sense?

The journey towards knowledge and understanding is a defining characteristic of humankind - or at least we think it should be. The beautiful thing about this journey is that it's fractal: with each layer of understanding you uncover, you find yourself staring at another new field of knowledge as recognisably complete but as mysterious as the last layer, before discovery. In fact, we'd even suggest that knowledge might be exponentially fractal: uncovering the next stratum of new knowledge seems to unearth a whole other dimension of knowledge to learn. The more you discover, the more you reveal how incomplete and minuscule your knowledge is.

To learn, you have to have mastered listening. Once you've done that, being open to learning is often as much about not being afraid of being in uncharted territory and being patient with the lack of knowledge you have, as it is to be able to let go of old ideas that you've held dear in the face of new compelling evidence, then junking that idea when another view eclipses that last certainty. Of all the provocations in this book, this is the only one that not only has no answer, it has no end. The techniques and stories we'll share in this chapter are just a glimpse of how we struggle with this compelling life-task. So are you up for the journey?

NITIN SAWHNEY

Nitin Sawhney is a producer, songwriter and DJ. His work combines Asian and other worldwide music influences with elements of jazz and electronica and often explores themes such as multiculturalism, politics and spirituality. He has scored for and performed with orchestras, and collaborated with and written for the likes of Paul McCartney, Sting, The London Symphony Orchestra, Ellie Goulding, and Nelson Mandela. Performing around the world, he has achieved an international reputation across every possible creative medium. Often appearing as Artist in Residence, Curator or Musical Director at international festivals, Nitin also works extensively in musical education.

B&A: How often do you think you're wrong?

NS: I don't think in terms of dichotomies. I think in terms of being 'in tune' or 'out of tune'. For example, I don't believe in morality. Right and wrong is very much based on dichotomies that are set up, in my perspective, by people in power who are more often than not men who are top of the hierarchy they've devised themselves. The weak or deprived are put into a position where they feel guilty. Right and wrong is very much about guilt. So as a musician, I either feel I am 'in tune' or 'out of tune' with myself, and I may have to then retune my instrument when I'm in a different context, like a musician in a band.

B&A: How do you manage that when people are critical of something you do?

NS: I will listen and I will try to understand their perspective on it. I will try to find what they feel. I will ask them questions, and see if it actually benefits my expression in some way. I'll play my album to someone, and if they say 'I don't like this about it' I will think 'does that help me clarify my expression to myself? Does that help me find a more pure way of crystallising the thought?'

B&A: What role does surprise play in your work?

NS: I think it's important to play with expectations of yourself. I used to try and do one thing every month, which is out of character for me, so in a way I would try to simulate surprise in myself. I have a fear of heights so I did a trapeze course. I have arachnophobia so I'd push myself to have a spider on my arm. I'd do things every now and then, which were out of character. I remember reading 'The Dice Man' and this idea of randomizing possibility in terms of things that you do so actually that he would throw a six and be Jesus Christ for the day, do that and follow through. I like the idea of surprising yourself in your work and your creativity. Bringing in random elements where you can bring yourself harmonically to go to a different and unusual place rhythmically or melodically: sometimes you simulate that to throw your head in a new direction.

B&A: Are there any of your points of view that are radically different now than in the past? What are they?

NS: I spend more time trying to understand the nature of people who make me feel uncomfortable. For example, I'll try to understand racists, whereas years ago I would have just been angry. It is still difficult for me to overcome childhood issues I have, but then I think at the same time, I want to understand the mindset of people who are, in my point of view, fearful and spreading fear. I want to understand why they'd want to do that because I can't see it myself. It's a different way of thinking: I can't believe people are malicious in the first instance for no reason.

B&A: Was there a moment that led you to decide that that's the way you were going to see it?

NS: After I did 'Beyond Skin' because that exorcised a lot of demons. After I did 'Prophecy' that was about me going around the world and trying to understand how it is that people have actually been overlooked: invisible people, like Aborigines, or street kids in Brazil, people who have been historically undermined and asking them directly how they feel. Nelson Mandela is someone who has forgiven a lot. When I interviewed him in his home I wanted to understand how or why he came to that point.

B&A: Do you think you can learn creativity?

NS: Yeah. I am a patron of an organization where we teach different ways of being creative to kids. I think that a musician is a musician before they've even picked up an instrument, when they pick up that instrument they can hear themselves speaking.

B&A: So it's about finding the channel, method or vessel that suits you as an individual?

NS: Yeah, I think that's the thing. I knew as soon as I saw a piano I knew it was a very important part of my voice. I kept running up to it and hitting it and trying to figure out how to get it to work the way I imagined it should. I knew there was something valid there I needed to understand.

B&A: Is there anything in particular you wish you knew more about?

NS: Oh man, just about everything! There's very few things I wish I didn't know more about. That's it, I have a really strong interest in maths and physics. I wish I knew a lot more about them. I am not conventionally religious or anything so it's the closest I can get... I believe in trying to find answers and evidence to real questions. Physics holds a lot of information about how things work and where we are in the flow or everything. If I could understand a bit more about the flow that would be great but I don't want to know the mind of God, I never would. That's like bacteria trying to understand why I'm here eating Nandos - it doesn't make sense! All I am trying to understand is where my place in the flow of everything is. Creativity is about that.

B&A: Your focus is music in the broadest sense. Do you think it is as clear to most people where they are best placed?

NS: I don't know, I really hope so. I think you can sense when people are fighting the flow and fighting themselves. I think intuition is programmed to tell us where we're at in terms of flow and if we fight it, it makes us feel discordant and unable to cope. I think about doing other things, all the time, and I do other things: I've written plays, I draw, I do mental arithmetic. I was an accountant. I've done all types of things! I get bored if I'm doing one type of creativity all along because then I think I'm trapped in the form rather than the expression. By doing lots of things, you freshen up and it keeps you thinking.

B&A: Nitin, which provocation out of them all resonates most with you?

NS: I think it's 'The work you do best is the work you love is the work you do best.' I mean for me, I don't really think in terms of work, although other people will define what I do as work. For me, it's a passion so I've always believed if you follow your passion then you'll end up in a really good place and you're at your most productive. It also depends who you're trying to please: for me the best place to start is myself... It always has to start with passion from a personal perspective. When I'm creating anything, whether creating music, lyrics or writing, it has to come from a place of passion and real need to express something that feels like it wants to come out: that's what I love and is where I am most happy because I feel like I am in a state of being in communion with a universal flow.

B&A: How do you balance that with the need to answer a brief?

NS : It's interesting because you know, I have to put myself into a different mindset. For example, when I'm working, I always ask myself where am I on the line between personal catharsis and communication? For example, if I'm working with someone else I have to take them into account as well. If they are making a film, or communicating to a large audience, I firstly still have to look within myself to find something cathartic but that still resonates with where they are coming from otherwise I can't help them.

B&A: So to say 'yes' to a project you have to figure out if that's possible before?

NS : Yes, that's very well-observed. From the starting point I have to have long conversations with whoever it is to work out where we can collaborate, where we can resonate together and find common ground and how we work in a symbiotic way.

on nigerian petrol pump attendants

This is a story about a phenomenon I noticed in 1999 when I first visited Nigeria. It describes why change is difficult, even if the alternative is blindingly, obviously better.

There was an election on. Olu Falae and the former general Olusegun Obasanjo were contesting the first presidential election in sixteen years. One of Obasanjo's election promises, I heard, was that under his leadership he'd get Nigeria's petrol flowing.

At the time of the election Nigeria had an economy which the BBC described as being in "abject decay". Their oil boom of the 1970s was ancient history, but even so, Nigeria's oil industry still had the potential to make it one of Africa's richest, most self-sufficient and powerful nations. Instead, back in 1999 a drive through Lagos saw frequent queues for the pumps as rickety supply lines, corruption, poor management and an emphasis on exporting oil to earn precious foreign currency meant that, at worst, commuters had to park their cars outside petrol stations overnight to ensure their supply of gas.

To me, a promise to get the petrol flowing was a big promise indeed.

I asked friends in Lagos whether they believed Obasanjo's promise. Surprisingly, their answer tended to be a wry shrug. After a few too many of these, I plucked up the courage to ask why the shrug? Didn't they believe he could do it? Didn't they believe he'd try? Did they just think he'd salt away any upside for himself? The answer was both simpler and more intriguing:

They told me it wouldn't necessarily be a good thing.

When I probed further, here's how it was broken down to me:

When you queue for petrol, the lady who's pumping gas is a strong woman indeed. You drop her a few extra Naira, she's got a way to give you an extra couple of squirts of gas off the meter. If the petrol's flowing, what's she to do?

And if the queue lasts all day or all night, you can normally pay someone to mind your car for you. What are they to do if the petrol flows? They'll have to find a living elsewhere.

And what of the market of boys selling you stuff through your car window while you wait. It's dangerous work walking the highways in a go slow, plying your trade. In a petrol queue, you're a safe, captive audience. What will they do? Where will they go?

You see, this "petrol flowing" business. It's not all good.

And that's the Nigerian Petrol Pump Attendant Syndrome.

It's a syndrome with good news and bad news. First the good news: people are by nature positive and resourceful. No matter how dysfunctional a system may seem to be, people find function in it, and make the system work for them.

But here's the bad news: This resourcefulness builds in vested interest – no matter how inequitable, illogical or downright perverse it may be. These vested interests make systems profoundly difficult to change.

But how do you achieve change in similarly entrenched environments?

There's so much to learn exploring places like the forecourts of Port Harcourt. Having worked in approaching fifty countries, we are often in new, unfamiliar environments. We've found we have to dig deep, talk to real people, get inside local culture and try to see the hidden logic of a situation that reveals what's really going on and all that can stand in the way of change (no matter how apparently illogical or counterintuitive). Only then can we completely understand a problem and start finding ways the problem can be solved.

on what you learn when you learn to make an omelette

How do you know when you've learned something? I mean, not just attended the class and diligently taken notes, but truly absorbed what you've been taught? Remembering back to something that happened to me many years ago reminded me that I believe there are three stages to true learning: experiencing, trying and teaching. Together these three elements not only keep learning as a circular journey, they keep it social.

To truly learn, you have to share.

One night, back when I was about 19, I found myself as one of a small number of stayers at a late-night house party. We'd all been drinking and smoking (the kind of things I did back then) and were all getting a bit peckish (in embarrassingly Cheech and Chong-like style, the term we used back then was "we had the munchies"). I suggested that I'd make omelettes for everyone. I went to the kitchen, found a big pan and some eggs and set to work. I came back and offered my leathery, eggy handiwork to a friend called Carlton.

"You don't know how to make an omelette, do you Andrew?" said Carlton after his first mouthful. "Yes I do. What do you call that?" I rebutted defensively. "Er, I'd call it 'not good'. Let me show you how to make a good omelette." Carlton replied as he stood up and made his way to the kitchen, leading me with him.

He started to explain: "Okay, crack two eggs in a bowl. Now add a tablespoon of water - eggs are slightly too thick on their own. Now mix until its one colour. No trace of yolk or white showing." He continued. "Now add a bit of salt and pepper."

I added salt and pepper, then reached for the big pan. "No, too big. Grab that one about the size of a 45 record." I complied and put the smaller pan on the hob and then reached for the oil. "No, never oil. Always butter." I put the oil back and put a knob of butter into the now hot pan.

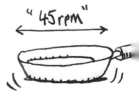

"Now listen". He said. I listened. Carlton was silent.

"Well I'm listening; say something". I blurted eventually. "Not to me, listen to the butter. Can you hear it sizzling?" I listened. I could.

"Right now wait until you can't hear it any more. It stops sizzling when all the water's evaporated. From then you've got about five seconds until the butter starts to burn." A couple of seconds after a raised eyebrowed look between us confirmed the buttery silence, Carlton said "okay, put the mix in now."

I poured the eggs in the pan and watched them bubble and curl at the edges of the pan. Almost instantly, Carlton delivered his next instruction "Right, now fold the edges into the middle, then swish the mix round so it covers the pan again, Now watch the omelette." He went on, "It's cooking, but it's still wet on the top. When some, not all, of that wetness has cooked away, fold it onto the plate. It'll finish cooking on the plate." I did what Carlton asked and folded the hot, soft, slightly browning omelette onto the plate.

Now, up to this point I don't think I had done any learning at all. The first third of my learning was about to take place.

With Carlton smiling beside me, I dug my fork through the soft, steaming eggs on the plate, then lifted the forkful into my mouth. It tasted wonderful. Carlton's instructions worked. Using this method, I made omelettes for everyone that night. Munchies abated, we gradually drifted home.

But that was only one third of my learning journey. The second third came a couple of days later. Without Carlton looking over my shoulder, I made omelettes for my housemates. I flew solo and landed, not just safely, but perfectly. The last third was when I had to show my housemate, Annie, how to make this sumptuously simple meal. I taught her as I'd been taught, and passed the method on. I truly knew I understood what Carlton had taught me only once I had taught it to someone else.

Experience, try, teach. Once shared with others my learning was complete. Of course, having to test what you've learned by teaching is a bit scary, right? But for us, it's the ultimate test and after all, you can't make an omelette without breaking eggs.

NOTES:

3. THERE'S A WORLD OUTSIDE YOUR MANOR AND I WANT YOU TO SEE IT

When it comes to writing great words, the name "Dylan" seems to be a winner, whether as a first or surname. There's Bob, there's Thomas, and there's Kwabena Mills, better known by his nom de plume, Dizzee Rascal. It's from his 2007 hit, World Outside that we take this chapter's provocation. Dylan has this to say:

Running around hype and criminal antics fed me for a while
But studio gave me a lot more creative style
And took me to another world beyond the estate
Some kind of haven from the beef and some of the stress, mate
I wouldn't call it no escape, the roads are in my heart
Making it that more difficult for me to climb the chart (for real)
But it's the sacrifice I made, it's all good, star
Same reason I ain't always in the hood star
I do my thing, you know I'm grafting like I always was
It just ain't quite like it was, simply cause

I know there's more than this, man
There has to be more than this, man
Nah, there's gotta be more than this, man
Standardly there's gotta be somewhere other than this, man

[Writer: Dylan Kwabena Mills, Copyright: Hero Music Ltd.]

This chapter's all about the curiosity and bravery that make up Dylan's dare - get out, find new stuff, don't forget what you're about or where you're from, but learn to see anew and learn to grow and find new "creative style" of your own.

CHARLIE
DARK

Charlie Dark is one of London's most important cultural innovators. His career started as one third of Attica Blues a early signing to James Lavelle's Mo' Wax label. He's been behind seminal musical explorations ever since - as an accomplished producer and remixer and, live, setting up ground breaking events such as Blacktronica, Black Atlantic at the Studio Museum Harlem, MyChoons and The Accidental Powercut. Above that, Charlie's an acclaimed performance poet, educator and runner, setting up the Nike-backed running collective, Run Dem Crew in 2008: this season they are over 300 strong and have seen many thousands of young runners pass through their doors since 2008.

B&A: If there's one thing that we think defines you as a creative, it's curiosity. So why do you start so many new things?

CD: Ha ha ha! I start new things out of frustration. Frustration drives me. That's the reason I start so many new things.

B&A: Is it frustration with something in you, or something you find in the world around you?

CD: It's a combination between the two. For instance, the reason I started Run Dem Crew was that I was frustrated with the idea that something so amazing as running had so many barriers around it. The reason I started Blacktronica was I was frustrated in myself because there was something I understood inside, and a small circle of people around me understood, but the people who needed to understand it (to make it commercially viable) didn't understand it. But that's a problem that's always going to be there.

B&A: Why's that?

CD: You're normally too ahead of the mainstream. You're trying to tune into pirate radio when the rest of the world is on mainstream commercial but you have to fine tune to listen to pirate radio. But the mainstream doesn't want to live with the static and interference! I'm quite happy to have interference.

B&A: So do you seek out frustration because it's a creative driver?

CD: I like that and I will work with that! Yeah, definitely. I like to problem solve. My life path has brought problems to my doorstep. If I don't deal with solving the problem, no one else will.

B&A: But if you see someone else doing work where they see a cultural problem to solve, to what extent would you be interested in following them (as opposed to you being a pioneer?)

CD: As I get older, I'm more open to solving problems with other people. But I'd want mine to be a better version! The hip-hop inside me drives me to improve what's already there. You can't emulate, you've got to make something bigger and greater and that's very important to me. That's one of my frustrations. A lot of people are happier to replicate what's already successful instead of remixing it.

B&A: I guess that the frustration is as well as a curious creator, you have to be an explainer or translator too?

CD: Yes. This can be frustrating particularly when you go higher up the decision-making food-chain because there's less imagination at the top. If we were outside talking with some young people about some amazing new phone you were going to create that could project onto walls and do crazy stuff, the kids would say "yeah, yeah! when can we do that?!" Whereas, as you get more experienced, you get to people for whom the idea is not enough. Risk assessment starts. They ask "if I take this idea on, will I lose my job?" When you start you're not thinking about repercussions, you're just thinking about doing the idea.

B&A: But doesn't this hem you in too, Charlie? As you get older you do have more to lose?

CD: Yeah, most definitely. This is the dilemma I find myself in: what am I going to expend my energy on?

B&A: Is that about being able to look back at the things that have gone wrong when you might have wasted your time?

CD: No, I never look back and think I've wasted any time. Everything I do has given me a life experience that I can add to the next thing that comes along.

B&A: Do you learn those things at the time, or is it a slow burn?

CD: A mixture of both (laughs). Some mistakes you have to make over and over again before you get them into your head!

B&A: The cliché runs that you learn more from your failures than your successes. But can you share something you've learned from a success?

CD: I learned a lot from the success of Run Dem Crew. I learned about community and how community builders come in all shapes and sizes. I realised that I've always been part of a community. Back when I was making music, I was part of a community then but I lost sight of this. Run Dem Crew has restored my sense of community.

B&A: How do you think social media has affected this? Do you think that communities form more easily with these tools, or do you think it is more difficult, because there's an illusion of community?

CD: I think as far as long-term sustainable communities are concerned, social media has had a bad effect. The online community has a boredom-threshold related shelf-life. Because there's no incubation period, the community isn't founded on any shared principles, values or vision of where it's heading before it goes public.

B&A: And in terms of learning from failures?

CD: That would be the African Beats project. It just didn't work in the way I thought it would. I thought I'd curate and create this hybrid of African and electronic music but realised: 1) it wasn't my job and 2) under the circumstances I was working and because of who I was working with, it could never have worked because it wasn't embedded in a community. I tried to get all these disparate characters together, then another organisation that doesn't really understand is going to sell and promote it. People came but there was no legacy. So now, when I go along to South African music like Okmalumkoolkat I think to myself, you're actually doing a much better job than I did!

B&A: Is this to do with your African Beats project being "top down", as opposed to "bottom up" creativity?

CD: Yes, there was definitely a "top down" thing going on. It taught me a way not to work. As people who are natural influencers start stuff in reaction to the mainstream or the establishment, they need to protect their thing as it starts to grow. They need to protect it from the very thing we set up to be against. What happens too often is we set up alternatives but really we want to be accepted by the big thing and as soon as the mainstream looks round and gives you approval, you move to them. Do this and before you know it you lose your power and your influence and lose sight of the thing you set up to be. You get bought and you get shackled. You lose the agility that's one of your core strengths. Independents need to keep asking the question: are you a ninja or are you a sumo wrestler?

B&A: This kind of curiosity and exploration is risky. What's the biggest risk you ever took?

CD: Starting to run. That's because it alienated me from my music community that didn't. It was the same when I decided to stop DJing for a while. That was a very big risk that was partly financial but also community is safe and you know it. I've never really had a problem with risk. If you grew up as a black male in the UK in the 80's, you're used to being an outsider. Some people change themselves to fit within the system, some people straddle and others defiantly remain who they are. I've done all three.

B&A: So which is your favourite?

CD: It's definitely to be on my own. At one point I was definitely a man who tried to straddle both worlds but now I'm more interested in being an individual, being an outsider and being myself. Because if you don't it confuses other people, because they don't know where you stand. The more successful you become and the more you get recognised as being someone who has ideas, the more you get approached for ideas by people who you set your work up to oppose. That's why it's very important for me to say "this is what I do, if you want to work my way, then we're cool, otherwise I'm not interested." And that's a frightening place to be.

explain it to your mum

A TOOL TO TEST YOUR IDEAS

NOBODY knows you like your Mother does. No one else will ever be as HONEST with you: She won't just tell you what you WANT to HEAR!

① CALL YOUR MUM
The conversation is going to be an acid test for how clearly defined your idea is.

It's good to TALK

② EXPLAIN your idea using SIMPLE language & layman's terms. You'll find it helps expose the CLARITY of your thinking

it's err.... um.. well..... er... ? ? ? ? ? ?

③ LISTEN to the feedback you get. It will be INSTANT, HONEST & could highlight areas you haven't yet thought of (Even if mum isn't the intended audience)

LISTENING as a GROUP lets everyone hear the feedback DIRECTLY
+ it's also VERY FUNNY!

YOUR GAME HERE

NOTES:

4. BE THE PERSON EVERYONE WANTS ON THE TOUR BUS

When I was a drummer, I was a bit of a pain in the arse. I was a great drummer, but I was a bit too, let's say... "restless". I loved all of the preparation that went into setting a band up. I loved naming the band, picking the musicians, choosing, writing, rehearsing and recording the songs, then working out what to do - I loved the strategy, basically.

As I was organised and (relatively) smart, I quickly found myself in demand as a musical director to do this stuff, then go out on tour with the band. Unfortunately, that's often when my interest waned. I didn't like the touring. It just seemed a bit repetitive. For me it wasn't the creative bit, so I ended up bored and a bit chippy. I picked fights and argued the toss. Too late I learned that being able to play and having core skills wasn't enough. How I acted was way more important. Every musician who's auditioned can likely play their instrument. So that's not the important bit. What's more important is whether you're the kind of person the band wants (and wants to keep) on the tour bus.

Almost everybody says they look to hire "nice people". But what does this mean? Of course, building and maintaining relationships is vitally important - especially as that percussionist you're dissing today could be the record producer you're begging to record you tomorrow. Being able to empathise with others, then being sensitive to group dynamics is core to fostering trust, honesty and healthy working environments that can improve any business you're in. This chapter's about that stuff. Ben would have put the provocation that names this chapter a little more indelicately, his title would have been "Don't be a dick".

KWAME
KWATEN

Kwame has been a musician, record producer and music industry consultant since the 1980's. He was a member of D-Influence who self released their first album after a plug from Tim Westwood. D-Influence soon became a production group, producing and remixing work for Mick Jagger, Seal, Jay-Z and more. Kwame's experience and portfolio puts him at the top of the UK's music business experts. In 1996 he started the Urban Music Seminar, bringing aspiring black and urban musicians together with top industry professionals, regularly selling out London's Royal Festival Hall. Subsequently, he started The Ultimate Seminar in partnership with Westminster University.

B&A: When you're hiring people as a manager, have you thrown someone off the bus or tour because they couldn't fit in or didn't have the right attitude?

KK: Yes. Absolutely. I'll nix that stuff before it even reaches the tour bus. I'll just politely suggest that maybe that person isn't the right person. "Be the person everyone wants on the tour bus?" To me out of all your provocations, this one's almost too obvious to comment on. It's like saying "I'm black". Who's going to argue with that? You can't have been in the music industry since you were 18 - so way more than half your life, and then some - and not be the person everyone wants on the tour bus. Because if you're not, you can't last. Because the thing is, the more time goes on, the more transparency there is about who you are and what you do.

B&A: Is it that the more people know you or the less you can pretend?

KK: With human beings generally, a really shifty geezer could probably hide whoever they are for about three years. They've got three years, maximum. By the end of the third year (at the very latest) people around start to notice the repeating patterns and say: "you know what?

you're fished out!" In the music business, this might be why if you see an artist, or a chair or an MD or executive who lasts longer than three years, it's probably the real thing.

B&A: When someone's young, what gets them to the the point when they're able to collaborate and work better with others? Is it better empathy or better self-knowledge? Is it more important for them to be able to understand others or understand themselves?

KK: It's both but I think you have to have a very strong understanding of who you are because you can't be "tour bus you" all the time. Even the most happy-go-lucky person in pressure cooker work environments needs to know their rhythms and be able to see their darker times, and find time for themselves. It's as if you need an hour's worth of personal time to be able to do 11 hours of time with others. It's really essential.

B&A: As a manager, have you seen people who you think could go either way with their attitude (so it could improve to the point when they're an asset or continue on a downward path so you'll need to move them on)? In these cases, what do you do to help them to become their better self?

KK: I'm terrible. I just cut them. I've got to look at it like an equation. The amount of time I need to spend to get this person to where they need to be plus the urgency of having a band that needs to go out on tour divided by the time we've got (because sometimes, it's not about the "right" it's about the "right now") equals they've got to go. Because, when I do that sum, then I think, you know what, I've got five other people I need to think about and they're working out. You're the sixth, you're expendable. I can find 15 people who won't give headaches - so "I love ya, but later!" The thing that makes this clearer is that as a manager, I'm not doing it for me. If I was doing it for me, I might take a little extra time, and I do (for instance with people who are working on the Seminars). But as a manager, I have to work in the best interests of my artist and make those kind of hard decisions.

B&A: You touched on the education seminars. You've dedicated a lot of your time and energy to them for years. What took you in this direction? Where did they start?

KK: Like with all D-Influence things, we just did it. Two gigs into our career, and out of the rehearsal room and we're supporting Michael Jackson. We were always about baptisms of fire! Urban Music Seminar was born out of me waking up at 4am one night and thinking: we've got this scene, with great music in it, but not enough people were talking about it. Everyone was waiting for someone else to put it into a business form. We also knew that something was wrong. There was no structure if you wanted to be something other than a singer or a performer. There was no place to learn outside of books. The one thing we knew about was entertainment. We wanted to educate by entertaining. Edutainment. You were coming to school, but it was like coming to a gig.

B&A: And the role I saw you play at Urban Music Seminar was itself very theatrical. I saw you slag off audience members for asking crap questions.

KK: Straight up! And I still do this at the Ultimate Seminar that I run.

B&A: Are you having a go at them for asking a poor question, or are you kind of having a go at a younger version of you?

KK: Definitely both. The only way you can even suggest that kind of thing is if you recognise the earlier you. That's the only way you can justify saying "that's a crap question". British audiences like to be informed. They like to be informed and have the rules of engagement laid out. That was also something we did with the Urban Music Seminars and still do with the Ultimate Seminars - we used to tell the young people who would come along and see Jay-Z or Damon Dash or Diddy "If you have someone sitting next to you who's talking all the way through, you have my permission to tap them on the shoulder, call them an idiot and tell them to get out. Or, if when it's question time you stand up and sing, and think that will impress and this is the right forum for that, we'll throw you out!".

B&A: What were you like when you were the age of the kind of person who attends a seminar, and what, if anything, has changed?

KK: I still have the thirst for knowledge I had then but I have to because whatever lessons you learned two years ago are now obsolete. It's a lot more dynamic than it was then. When I was a kid, the thirst was about going, watching, consuming. I'd go and watch seven bands in a night then go and watch another three. Without realising what I was doing, I was building up a vast database of what to do, what not to do and how to do it. So when it came to stagecraft, I had loads of this knowledge in my cells.

B&A: Are kids as hungry now?

KK: Some are. And some, because of the technology that's at their disposal are way ahead of anywhere I was at their age.

B&A: For young people how does the accessibility of technology, that means they can get started and work on their own easier, balance with the ubiquity of technology, which means there's a lot more competition than there ever was? Is it easier for a kid now, or more difficult?

KK: Easier on one hand because they have the tools to have a fluke out-of-the-box hit. More difficult because they have to replicate this success. Being able to replicate your one hit with another is the quantum leap. Have you got the dedication to do it again?

B&A: Dedication as opposed to skill?

KK: No, dedication. The skill is there if they've had a hit. The difference is their dedication to their craft, and their ability to find a team around them who can support them. This takes someone with experience to guide them in the right direction, and the artist's willingness to listen to them.

B&A: What's the advice you find yourself giving to young people again and again?

KK: It's the same advice our parents gave to us: work bloody hard; don't lie to others and yourself and try not to do anyone over.

B&A: You picked from our provocations "have a Californian optimism and a wry British sense of humour" as one that's important to you. If you were to add to that "and have a Ghanaian dot dot dot", what would that thing be?

KK: Ha ha ha! Great question. I think that thing would be Ghanaian manners. That's about respect. We don't have a fear of going to an older person and saying "tell us how to do this." or humbly asking "Can I be in the same room as you and learn from you?" That marketing-led idea that teenagers only talk to teenagers, or twenty somethings only talk to twenty somethings is nonsense. When Prince took me to one side when I came off stage after supporting him on tour, and said "I've got some advice for you", I'm THERE. Listening with all ears. When I came out of that tour, he'd schooled our arses. And it's no surprise that two years later D-Influence won the "Best Live Act Award" - because I'd listened!

MELANIE CHISHOLM

Melanie Chisholm, better known as Mel C, is a singer-songwriter, actress, and businesswoman. As a solo artist, Chisholm has sold more than 12 million records and been nominated for BRIT and ECHO awards. With the Spice Girls she toured the world and sold over 100 million records worldwide. Melanie was nominated Best Actress in a Musical at the 2010 Laurence Olivier Awards and Outstanding Newcomer at the 2010 Evening Standard Theatre Awards after her role in Blood Brothers. She is currently judging "Asia's Got Talent 2015".

MC: Well, I think with there being a tour bus involved, that's something I have a lot of experience in, but I don't really agree with your provocation. For me this is about the whole 'life learning' of yourself. I think we're conditioned to be what we think we should be, whether it's being a child and having peer pressure or whether it's doing the things your parents want you to do so that you feel that they love you. All of these pressures are things we put on ourselves. Personally the thing I struggle with is that when the defences are down any insecurity will start to confuse me. I start thinking 'who am I?' I am human and I want to do the right things, but every now and then I'll be doing what I am doing to win the approval of somebody else, or trying to be the person someone else wants me to be. But even then I'll be projecting that onto them – I don't know what they expect me to be!

B&A: You end up going in a circle and trying to second guess them?

MC: Yeah. So rather than having that situation, you need to just be. Just be.

B&A: How long does that take to learn?

MC: I'm still learning. It's a life long thing. Every now and again I feel like I'm almost in step with myself and in step with my soul. I think 'you're on the right track, you're on the right track' and something, even if it's just one afternoon, will throw you off course. We all want to be liked, but personally for me, I want to make people laugh, so I'll be the joker one afternoon and then afterwards I'll think 'oh I didn't really like the way I behaved in that scenario.' And so it's about pulling yourself back in line and not conforming to being what you think people expect you to be.

B&A: It's interesting because there's a dynamic there. I wanted to talk about empathy, but what you're talking about could be where a danger of empathy lies. How do you have the right amount of empathy where you're considering other people enough but not losing yourself in that consideration?

MC: It's difficult. Empathy is such a wonderful and important trait in a human being, but not at the detriment of your own emotional health I suppose. A line has to be drawn if you find you are compromising yourself.

B&A: When you find yourself thinking 'I was trying a bit too hard' in certain situations, do you think it was because you were losing sight of yourself or because you yourself are changing as you age and grow, and are holding on to an 'older' self?

MC: All of our life experiences mould whom we become, but unfortunately when it comes to some of our life experiences we could do with keeping 'the experience we've had' but shedding the behavioural patterns that may have formed because of this experience. For example, if you were bullied at school, it may make you a people pleaser, therefore you compromise your own integrity. That is a habit that needs to be broken yet it is so hard when it is ingrained into you.

B&A: So, the defence mechanism outstays its welcome. You are in a new situation and you don't need that behaviour anymore. How does that affect how you put teams of people together around yourself? How long does it take for you to decide if you can invest trust and time into that person?

MC: Personally, I feel I've been lucky and I feel like there's a guardian angel that is taking care of things. I've gravitated towards good people, but of course, every now and then you get stung. When you're bound to people in your life who aren't a positive influence it is about learning how to manage that. Now we live in a society where friends have become the new family, so it's just having the courage to surround yourself with people who are good for you, and equally you are good for them. Also, you need to eradicate those who are surplus to requirements without being mean!

B&A: Is that about instincts or actual evidence and proof? Do you require people to demonstrate the trustworthiness that you're going to invest in?

MC: I think it is an instinct. For me, as soon as I meet someone I get a vibe and it's not always right, but generally that's what you've got to go on: it's human nature. It is about trusting yourself.

B&A: Does it get easier or more difficult as you get older?

MC: I think it gets easier, you put up with less (laughs).

B&A: Have you ever thrown anyone off the tour bus for not fitting in?

MC: (Chuckles). I've never thrown anyone off the tour bus, even though I've wanted to! My problem with tour buses is that most of my bands like to have a good old drink up after a show but I don't tend to drink much on tour because I'm singing and its not the best thing for my voice and my head!

B&A: When you're looking to put people around you who you're going to have to spend an awful lot of time with, to what extent, past their core skills, do you look for their other ways of being?

MC: Over the years, people have stayed and people have gone, sometimes someone with a great skill may go because they don't fit in as people. I think a happy ship is really important: I'm not interested in egos. When I'm on tour these days it's my show but I don't see it like that, I'm not more important than anybody else. We're a team, it is all about being equal and working together.

B&A: What are the biggest differences between being a solo artist and being part of a group?

MC: For me, it is so much easier to be the person who has the final decision on things. I mean I always have a close group of people who I will talk to but at the end of the day the decision is mine. When you're part of a band, in my experience, you work with people who can often have very different opinions to you. It becomes quite exhausting always having to compromise and be diplomatic and I'm a diplomatic person! Everyone has a role and there are certain things I'd leave to someone else, and then there are certain things I need to be the boss of.

B&A: How long does it take when you're in a group to find or learn those natural roles?

MC: It takes two years I think to know somebody. The first year is all a bit 'ooh' and 'aah' getting to know each other but once that year has passed the pretence is dropped and that's when you know, you start to figure it.

B&A: Do you think you have unique qualities, or do you think anyone could do or follow the career that you've had?

MC: I think I have been very fortunate, but it feels like a jigsaw piece or a cog in a wheel of something pre-destined. We are all special. I think everybody has wonderful qualities and talents and it is just about whether in this lifetime they are able to fulfil or discover them. I think you have to work hard to be successful; I've certainly worked hard, and maybe that is one of the things people don't realise.

B&A: What is the biggest risk you've taken career-wise? Seeing you in Blood Brothers I was very impressed and that move was very brave.

MC: The funny thing is that Blood Brothers was the most terrifying thing I've done in my career but I had to do it. I had no choice. No one was making me do it but it was something I had to do for me. I was being guided to do it. It was a gift and opportunity that landed on my lap. I'd never done anything like that since school but I went out, took that deep breath and went on that ride.

how to learn
a lot of names

or HOW TO LOOK LIKE YOU CARE ABOUT PEOPLE (even if you don't!)

The trick is, there is no trick. The only way to do it is with PRACTICE

(A) IF MEETING someone  FACE to FACE for the 1st time:

(1) SAY HELLO & find out their name

Hi, I'm Bob. & I don't have a TV.

Ah, BOB, that face, no TV

(2) ALSO FIND OUT a little bit about them

then REMEMBER their NAME alongside their UNIQUE FACE & interesting story

(3) REPEAT with all the new people you meet individually

IF you're in a MEETING draw a quick table plan during introductions.

Andrew's record is 62 people in 1 afternoon!

If you know people's names you can PERSONALISE your message

B IF YOU'RE MEETING
A group of people

& you know about it in ADVANCE:

① GET PHOTOS of each
person before hand

(Google them if necessary)

② PRINT the photos & memorise
by playing games such as
Who's Who or Pelmanism

③ WHEN YOU MEET THEM
play game Ⓐ to ⟹
confirm & cement.

It's good to double check as
some people may have grown a
beard, dyed their hair, or
even aged horribly!

? ? , ? ? ? ?   WHEN you've got a LOT of names to remember
They're all individuals, so you only need
to remember ONE NAME at a time — THEIRS!

NOTES:

5. HAVE A CALIFORNIAN OPTIMISM AND A WRY BRITISH SENSE OF HUMOUR

To be able to see from someone else's point of view, it's helpful to know your own (initial) point of view. Looking at yourself, working out who you are, what you love, what you hate, what you're great at and what you're crap at is a first step to complementing your natural way of being. This can mean internal efforts to balance your prevalent, natural tendencies, or finding others around you who can do the balancing for you (and more likely a bit of both). Before Ben and I set up Ben&Andrew we were coached by Caroline Whaley. Of all the excellent advice she gave us, one piece has stood us in good stead: "Andrew, you're naturally gregarious; Ben you're naturally reflective. If you can use this mix right, you'll fly. But get it wrong and it'll break you."

So being receptive to other ways of seeing calls on deep self-knowledge, but it's nothing without the humility and flexibility to see other complementary points of view. We think it's only with this breadth and balance (between optimism and skepticism for instance) that you can have perspectives that are sufficiently broad to effectively solve problems.

There's another point. It was the Irish writer and wit George Bernard Shaw who is most often attributed as saying "England and America are two countries separated by the same language". Anyone who's spent any time in both the US and the UK gets his point. Language is just a small part of culture. Armed with a common means of communicating, one can be lulled into forgetting that non-verbal interaction and deeper cultural nuances are often far more important than the words you choose to express yourself with. To quote Shaw again (he's always great value for this stuff) "The single biggest problem in communication is the illusion that it has taken place." Making yourself understood is a cultural business.

This chapter explores what it takes to know yourself and know others (both individually and culturally) so you can get the balance right as you hope for the best and prepare for the worst.

JAMES
BOWTHORPE

London-born filmmaker, activist, furniture maker and adventurer
James has circumnavigated the world on a bicycle in the name of
Parkinson's research in 2009 and broke the world record for it along
the way. He has exhibited film work at MACBA and ICA, worked for
the OSCE monitoring the first democratic elections in Kosovo and is
a research fellow at the Institute for Psychiatry in London. In October
2015, James will travel to Manhattan where he will build a boat from the
waste he finds in the city. He'll take the boat to the source of the Hudson
River at Lake Tear of Clouds high in the Adirondack Mountains and
then navigate his way back to Manhattan on his boat. The Hudson
River Project is an unprecedented journey, which will explore man's
relationship with nature from a perspective we rarely see – that of the
river which enabled the city to grow in the first place.

B&A: What do you think you learnt about yourself from biking around
the world that you couldn't have learnt by staying at home?

JB: It's a very unique position to put yourself in so you learn lots of
different things. I had to live with a constant time pressure for the
whole trip which was difficult (and not something I was used to) and
at the same time I was constantly questioning myself - why am I doing
this again?! The easiest thing would have been to give up, and I would
have had lots of excuses to give up that nobody would have blamed me
for. I guess I've always fancied myself as being quite resilient and so
the trip tested that assumption out. I realised I could do it. This gave
me a quiet confidence that I could do just about anything else too.

B&A: So if nobody was watching you, would you have completed it?

JB: Do you know the Hawthorne Theory? In a nutshell, this guy
Hawthorne did tests in a factory about how to improve productivity
by improving lighting in different parts of the factory. In one
section they bumped up the lighting by a certain wattage and the
productivity increased. In other they didn't increase the wattage but
the productivity still increased.

They realised that being observed made the workers more productive. Their daily jobs were dull and boring. Nobody paid them any attention. So when they did, they worked harder. It's kind of the same with me on my bike. Through social media people were watching. This was really important. If I'm honest, if I was doing it in isolation for no reason other than my own record I would have probably given up.

B&A: So, with no one looking, except your conscience, what are your core values?

JB: I have a central belief that I try to stick to in everything. That is that I want to do things that I really enjoy but that will also be useful for the rest of the world. Good for me and good for others.

At the same time I'm also trying to bring all of the many things I'm interested in into each project I do. I remember going to see the careers person at school at 15 and saying to him that I wanted to do this, this and this and they said 'well that's not going to happen!' 'You need to choose just one!' I didn't agree and still don't. So now I'm just trying to prove him wrong really - that's my whole life.

B&A: So what else other than that careers advisory experience helped you figure out your values?

JB: Well I think a lot of it comes from your childhood experiences. It's when you learn without realising it. It also comes from getting a bit weathered - putting yourself in uncomfortable situations - so you learn from them. This is especially important if you've grown up in a structured environment. A lot of people don't have the chance to break out of the structures around them. You have to remove yourself entirely to be able to think about yourself - and realise just how small you really are in the grand scheme of things. Often, if you are part of a big structure you feel as powerful as that structure, but really you are not. Barack Obama is a good example. He had lots of great ideas but he got into power and then couldn't do many of them. So it's good to be an outsider sometimes.

B&A: When looking at a new project, how do you balance the scale of challenge and possibility of success?

JB: To take on a challenge you have to believe you are going to succeed. You can't start off thinking that you are going to fail - because then you'd set yourself up to fail. You need a bit of healthy denial. I think balance is really hard to strike in anything, though. You have to gauge it with experience. With the Hudson River Project

I'm just piecing everything together. If I can break big projects into individual tasks, I can do anything.

B&A: So that's about a kind of cumulative confidence?

JB: Yeah I guess so. I mean, I'm not jumping off buildings am I?! It's slightly calculated, but there are a lot of unknowns. But in my head, because I've done this, this and this then I think any big project is possible.

B&A: What motivates you to take up a challenge?

JB: The Hudson River Project is all about bringing together all the subjects and questions I'm interested in into one place but not doing it in a vacuum so it can be shared. If I can share it with other people I can at least start a conversation about questions I've asked myself all my life. I might not answer them, but with climate change for example, there's currently really only one strong narrative about the issue. Why don't we have two or even 90? I want to start these conversations off in other people so new narratives can emerge. I could have gone and done this on my own and not told anyone. But that's not the point.

Challenges like building a boat from trash, then sailing it down the Hudson are difficult. So I don't really understand why people would do something like that without a set of reasons beyond just completing the challenge. I think the outcome should be greater than yourself. I'd want to cause ripples or waves, rather than just nothing.

B&A: When you were cycling, and it was tough, how did you motivate yourself?

JB: When it was really hard, I kept a mental image in my mind that combined the things I really like that have resonance to me. You have to motivate the parts of your brain that are really just like an animal. So for me it was sex and food. I would imagine my girlfriend was around the next corner with a plate of really nice flapjacks!

B&A: But were you not disappointed when you got round the corner and she was nowhere to be seen?!

JB: No, you just transfer it again. You put yourself at the back of your brain and let the bits of your brain that are interested in that and nothing else take over. It's sort of separating your brain into these areas. But it's only for difficult bits - like when you are cycling over a mountain range at night and you can't see beyond your headlight and what would make sense would be to stop and even the animal part of your brain is telling you to do just that. But if you have another goal over and above that, where you have to defeat that part of your brain that wants to sleep and eat and have sex, you need some tricks!

More generally, when things are difficult you almost need to be able to ignore the things that get in the way. It's to do with trying one path and if its blocked you go back and try another one and try not to be down about it. It's really good to have a sense of humour with these things. I'm very serious about my projects but if I took it too seriously then I would just be a wreck. What I do is pretty absurd. But that's partly why I do it. It makes me laugh. If you spend a lot of time on your own then you learn how to be good company to yourself. If you can't make yourself laugh then you're in trouble.

One thing on your provocation though: In California it's easy to be optimistic because the sun is always shining!

B&A: Of all the provocations, is there one which is most resonant?

JB: For me it's "the more I know the more I know I know fuck all". Because the more you see the whole the more you can see the parts you don't know anything about.

B&A: Is that something you encounter a lot?

JB: Yes. The Hudson River Project, for example, spills out into so many fields. Like water quality for example - I have to learn about that (even though I know nothing about it).

B&A: Can you learn it all?

JB: No! I don't think you can. But you have to give it a go. The best thing a formal education can give you is the tools to learn how to learn. And apart from that it's not a great deal of use!

B&A: Did you think with The Hudson River Project you would have to learn so much?

JB: I don't think I have to. But you have to at least have a basic grasp of the relevant subjects. You have to be able to understand the crucial parts. Really I'm a generalist but that's something I thrive on and I feel is important because there are so few generalists out there. People are required to specialise so much. It's useful and interesting to be more general, to have a wider perspective and point of view - because you can look at stuff from a different angle and bring new points of view. I really enjoy being a generalist.

KATHERINE RYAN

Katherine Ryan is a comedian, writer and actress - Canadian by birth and based in London. She has appeared on UK TV panel shows such as 'Mock the Week', 'Never Mind the Buzzcocks' and '8 out of 10 cats'. She won the 2008 Nivea Funny Women Award and was runner-up in the Amused Moose Laugh-Off competition. Since then, she has had acting roles in Channel 4's 'Campus' and BBC1's 'Episodes'.

B&A: Do you write for yourself or your audience?

KR: You have to write for yourself. One of the reasons that I have a career in this country is because I came here with my own authentic voice. In this industry people love to say, oh, he's the angry one, he's the camp one, she's the... I think the voice you adopt needs to be authentic - so that people see the truth in what you say. No matter what.

B&A: So truth is important in comedy?

KR: It's vital. The way that politicians work is that they tell lots of tiny little truths so you feel they are being truthful. But what's on the inside, what's at the core of what politicians are saying is such a lie. It's a lie decorated with meaningless little truths. But a comedian is the opposite. They tell lots of little lies like punchlines that didn't happen, but at the end of it there is a kernel of truth that really resonates with the audience. The lies are a way of telling the truth and helping the audience to see themselves in that truth - we hold a mirror to people.

B&A: Was there a moment when you realised you were funny?

KR: When I was a child I knew I could get out of trouble with my mother by making her laugh. It was a treat for me to stay up with my mum and watch 'The Late Show with David Letterman.' I loved it. I was probably only about 10 but I thought the comedy showed mental dexterity. Comedy was always valued in our house and I saw the effect comedy could have. It could lighten a situation that was very dark and it could bring people together. A lot of my family are Irish. I don't know if it's with the drinking or what but there were men in my family who would get drunk and be mean and the women would make that better by making jokes about it - to lighten it up. At the same time, if you wanted someone to play with you you had to come and sit at the table and be part of the conversation and be funny. That's how I got people's attention. Comedy was like a medicine. It made everything better.

B&A: So, what makes something funny?

KR: I like watching the way people's brains work. In the UK there is a guy called James Lancaster whose work is just so original and well written. It all makes sense and everything is tied up at the end by calling back to the start when he gets there. He creates this beautiful woven pattern through his show and he never leaves a joke unfinished. If you painted James's show in colour it would be this intricate mathematical beautiful pattern.

B&A: Can you be funny about anything?

KR: I think it can be disarming to be funny about difficult subjects and the truth in something like the experience of an abortion or cancer. I hate to sound like a Scientologist because I'm not but their manifesto about getting stuff out so that it doesn't plague you anymore is interesting. But you have to be respectful about the subject and you have to finish the conversation, you can't leave anything open ended. You have to find what's funny. It's like a treasure hunt. That's the fun of the panel shows like Mock the Week. They'll give you something like ISIS and say right, there you are: be funny with that. I'm like you're kidding me! You can do it. But you have to take a sneaky way around it.

B&A: How good are you at stopping a joke when you know it might be harmful?

KR: I haven't been successful at that in the past. I did hurt people and some people even wanted to kill me. But I still stand behind that joke. It wasn't cheap or hurtful if you understood it properly. I think there are clear boundaries. You can't be a misogynist right now in comedy at all. It's not tolerated. You can't really be "fattist" either. The list goes on. Some things just become culturally unpalatable for their time.

Rape is a subject that really upsets audiences. If you've never been raped then you don't know what it's like. You can have empathy but you can't have complete empathy. My friend Sara explained a really good rule: let's say you've got a joke about rape you want to tell and you think it is worthy of being told. If you can tell that joke in a room alone with someone and be prepared to deal with their reaction and still stand behind it and then you still want to tell it, then you should go and tell it. That's what I love about comedy. If you believe in something you can say it. But there will always be people who misunderstand.

B&A: Does being funny for a living make day to day life more or less fun?

KR: To be honest I'm a day to day happy person. I definitely have a Californian sense of optimism but I think it's because I have Lupus. I got it from my town. There is a petrochemical plant there that poisoned us all. But apparently you can't say that. The town's called chemical valley - it cannot be safe! A lot of auto-immune responses are triggered by stress and it was when I was really stressed that my Lupus was at its worst. So Lupus actually is a blessing because if I feel even a little bit stressed then I can feel it coming on. I guess I'm taking something really dark and making it a blessing. I love my Lupus! I've cured it! So I actually don't think my happiness is from comedy. A lot of comedians I know are hugely depressed. There was something that said that being a comedian makes you more likely to be a psychopath. And I date them so I know!

B&A: Do you think that being funny needs other people. Or can you be funny on your own, on a desert island? Can you be funny to yourself?

KR: Yes! I love being by myself that was another one of my mum's quotes - only boring people get bored. I love my own company. I love love love it. The silence and quiet of being by myself is wonderful. You have to be able to make yourself laugh if you want to be able to make other people laugh. I don't think I'm the funniest person in the world. I don't sit at home and laugh at myself all day but there are things I can't say out loud and I have to share with myself because of the time and place. On the same token there can be a guy who is really funny with his mates in a pub but who would never be able to do stand up comedy. So there are different ways of communicating humour. Ultimately being funny to yourself is all that counts. How sad would it be if you weren't funny to yourself.

B&A: Would you call yourself a North American or British comedian?

KR: I love Brits. I'm a British comic. I wasn't really a comic in Canada. I worked in Hooters and did some TV. I never thought it would be a career. I hate Californian optimism, yet i'm dripping in it. It's a way in for me. People think I'm different and weird but they are fascinated by me. I tend to be the gross weird crush. Being weird has given me my career. But I'm not intentionally weird. I'm just being myself. I always say to people that no matter what you do it is so tempting to (because media is designed to make us jealous of one another) to consume more stuff to change yourself to fit this thing that doesn't really exist and I really think that I struggled a lot until I just accepted my authentic self. As soon as I did that then my voice in comedy came out and people got it. That sounds cringy but it's really true. People who are themselves are attractive because you feel safe with them.

angels & devils

GREAT FOR CLEARING THE AIR & FINDING OUT WHERE
PEOPLE'S HEADS ARE AT

A LOT OF BAGGAGE gets in the way
when asking Q's + solving problems
This game helps get EVERYTHING out in the open

IT'S A
LICENSE to
be HONEST

1 DEVIL's
first:

WRITE DOWN ALL your
frustrations, niggles
& things that keep
you up all night

PUT THEM ON THE
WALL 1 by 1 + SHARE
THEM

D | A

2 ANGELS
next

WRITE DOWN ALL the
things that are brilliant,
exciting & keep you
coming to work.

PUT THOSE UP TOO,
& SHARE THEM

WHAT you MIGHT find is:
The ANGELS usually outweigh the DEVILS,
& the positives can help answer the negatives

YOUR GAME HERE ⟶

Taught to us by the
brilliant Chris Barez Brown
founder of Upping your Elvis

dreamers, builders, critics.

A GAME TO GIVE EVERYONE A VOICE & MOVE IDEAS FORWARD

① INSTEAD of seperate teams, dedicated to **1** task:

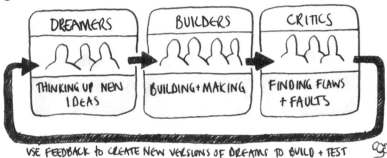

DREAMERS	BUILDERS	CRITICS
THINKING UP NEW IDEAS	BUILDING + MAKING	FINDING FLAWS + FAULTS

USE FEEDBACK to CREATE NEW VERSIONS OF DREAMS TO BUILD + TEST

....& Repeating until the water runs clear

② KEEP THE GROUP TOGETHER

and divide up TIME to focus the individual tasks. BE STRICT you can only do the task for the time zone you're in!

AND: Time to go round again & again

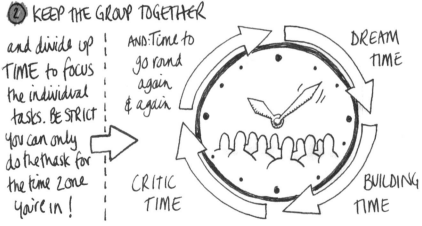

DREAM TIME

BUILDING TIME

CRITIC TIME

③ THIS WAY OF WORKING...

Gives everyone a voice

= Embraces diversity of approach

Moves ideas along whilst listening to ALL views

R GAME HERE ↰

on being "independent" (not "freelance") to assert your values

Of the 26 years work I did since I graduated until Ben and I formed Ben&Andrew, I was an employee for just six of them. The rest of the time I created my own work, or was an outsourced contractor for others. After a few years of working like this, I came to call myself "independent" and not freelance. I never really liked the term "freelance". "Freelance" seems to suggest a powerlessness with no values of ones own. When I found that the term came from Walter Scott's Ivanhoe to describe a mercenary (literally a "free lance"), that confirmed my suspicions. "Independent", on the other hand, suggests you bring values of your own to the party. Independence is about having your own goals, principles and issues you believe in and will fight for. Once asserted, this independence not only provides a compass of sorts - what work to take and who to work with, it also adds a degree of esteem. As an independent (not freelance) your value is your non-aligned, independent view.

So, I was independent, not freelance.

Done right, this positioning can allow you to lead your own agenda, do your own work and deliver your own value whilst still doing it in collaboration with others. But there's more: you can function with low overheads (for much of my independent life I worked from a shed at the end of my garden with no employees and minimal costs) and you can have an agility which can be a great advantage over larger competitors. As a master of your own timetable, you can better explore and learn from creative and cultural innovation, allowing you to change direction easily in response to new opportunities.

Many friends who work within larger businesses have said that they wished that this independence could be afforded to them from within their organisation. This is something we've tried to have as core to our approach at Ben&Andrew.

Another aspect of an independent work life that we've adopted at Ben&Andrew is the ability to proactively instigate our own ideas and projects. Again, this is very different from a "freelance" waiting for the phone to ring with the next gig. This not only provides the potential for new income streams, it changes the relationship with clients. Being able to go to a prospective client saying "I've got something I'm working on that I think you'll be interested in", is a very different call than "have you got any work?" It sets up the prospect of a more equal relationship from the start.

The most important aspect of working independently with your own values is it gives you license (or even an obligation) to do what you love so you can love what you do. This is the most important aspect of values-based independent working that Ben&Andrew tries to follow. We work hard to only do work that really interests and excites us. If you get this right, it's a virtuous circle. If you do the work you love; because you love it, you do it well; because you do it well, people ask you to do more work that interests and excites you.

Although being your own boss can mean having a boss that works you like a dog and who regularly wakes you with work matters in the middle of the night, that shouldn't also mean that you have to take work that you think is boring or uninspiring. Doing dull work puts you in an uninspiring place and that becomes where you reside.

So whilst the challenge to people working independently is how can you have enough structure to assert your values both in work and beyond, the challenge to organisations is the converse. For organisations, the question is how to foster independent spirits within their businesses, and fight off the "diseconomies of scale" that come as an organisation gets bigger, less agile and less proactive. This is the challenge we face at Ben&Andrew and will face as we grow. We'll let you know how we're getting on...

NOTES:

6. THE WORK YOU DO BEST IS THE WORK YOU LOVE IS THE WORK YOU DO BEST

The educator Ken Robinson starts his handy book "Finding Your Element" with an old story: "Two young fish are swimming down a river and an older fish swims past them in the opposite direction. He says 'Good morning, boys. How's the water?' They smile at him and swim on. Further up the river, one of the young fish turns to the others and says, 'What's water?'"

Finding a place that's so comfortably you, means finding a place that is so naturally home, you don't even know you're in it. But that's rarer than it should be. A friend who was departing the role as CEO of a high-status London advertising agency told us another aquatic tale: "The pressure of the job was so great. I felt like a frog being boiled. You know what they say - if you put a frog into hot water, it'll jump out and save itself, but put it in cold and gradually turn up the heat and it'll boil to death. I was not only the frog, I thought my job - my speciality even - was to withstand the scalding temperature!"

Just because you're good at something, it doesn't mean that's the right thing to do. We think a far better barometer of where you should place your energy, in work and in life, is to find the thing you love. If you can find this, you tend to do it better. And the feedback continues in a loop: doing work that you're best at is normally more enjoyable than being mediocre or even failing, so you love it more.

This chapter's provocation is about that quest: the search to find your element and do the best work by doing the work you love. Like our two interviewees, Martin and Maria, it might mean radically changing where you put your energy, but we believe it's worth it. Find your element and you'll not only transform your own happiness, you could transform the effect you're able to have on the world around you.

MARTIN
MORALES

Whilst heading Disney's music division in London, Martin launched High School Musical, Jonas Brothers, Miley Cyrus, Demi Lovato and Selina Gomez in Europe. All that was fun, but he knew he wasn't in his element... In his teens he worked as a silver service waiter, a barman and then as a DJ before starting his own events with food and music including the much loved Global Kitchen which featured a DJ playing records and cooking at the same time (him). Martin has always had a passion for cooking, so in 2010 he quit his job as Head of Disney Music, sold his house and decided to dedicate his life to food and culture from Peru. Ceviche was born.

MM: "The work you do best is the work you love is the work you do best" is basically my life ethos. I always knew I wanted to do something creative with my life - from being a painter, to working in graphic design, to working in interior design, to art direction. Music came in at the age of 19 when I started university. My inspiration was a need for escapism. When I came to the UK from Peru at the age of eleven I used to go and hunt down music in the local library in Coalville in Leicestershire. I'd go there, copy cassettes, listen to John Peel and learn about classical music, then Motown and hip-hop. I just worked through the sections.

B&A: What brought you to the UK from Peru?

MM: My father was threatened there by the guerilla movement "The Shining Path" and lost his job and my mother left my father for another man. He was British, so he decided to come home.

B&A: So you were an 11 year old Peruvian boy in Coalville, Leicestershire. What was that like?

MM: Horrible. I suffered racism left right and centre. All those words I don't want to say, they called me.

MM: Music was a relief and an escape. Music was something pure and beautiful.

B&A: Did you ever find your own crowd there?

MM: I moved to school in Loughborough, and that changed my life. It was a Catholic school, so there there were more ethnic minorities at that school. The friends I made there were into graffiti and breakdancing and judo and skateboarding. We were the local outsiders. I've always been an outsider from day one. I was born into a context of privilege in Lima, Peru. But I was an outsider there too, because my father was British and white, but my mother came from the Andes (and this world was very "real" - it brought me right back down to earth, because this part of the family was very humble). So even in Peru, I was very different to the kids at school there. The outsider friends in Coalville were looking at stuff that others didn't look at and listening to stuff that no one listened to. They were looking outside of Coalville for their inspiration.

B&A: When you're constructing your own identity as a young person, to what extent is it formed from within and to what extent is it shaped by the wider cultural assumptions of what you might be, or might be capable of?

MM: You make up what you are, but the society around you shapes how you interact with what you find locally. The racism I encountered made me avoid rock music (because I saw it as "white man's music"). The environment I was in made me censor certain cultural choices.

B&A: Was it something in your experience as a migrant - the act of coming from one place to another - that provided the impetus for your creativity?

MM: No, I think it's about the suffering. Pain creates an aggressive search for solutions. Desperation creates lateral thinking. It's the survival instinct that makes people look more broadly. Yes, its migration, but its what forces people to migrate - their mindset - draws the artist, the entrepreneur, the creative out of you.

B&A: So when did the cooking start?

MM: I'd always cooked. My mother had left, and my father didn't cook, so I had to learn. I was going to either eat shit food or good food! But I loved it, right back to when I was in Peru. I always had a fascination with food. In the UK, I used to cook for my friends - the breakdancers and those guys. I'd entice them to mine with food.

B&A: What was your first signature dish?

MM: I guess that would be one that ended up in my book: my great-aunt's chicken bolognese, that I called "Carmela's Chicken". It's one of the best home cooked soul food dishes in the world. She taught me a whole array of dishes just by watching her. I was always in the kitchen from about seven, shelling the pods, peeling the potatoes and just listening and taking it in.

B&A: But that wasn't the direction your career went.

MM: No. I studied Media and Spanish at University. All my mates were getting stoned, but I was into music from the beginning. I was always very entrepreneurial, always very proactive. I had a radio show, did gigs as a DJ and was doing PR for club nights. After I graduated I got a job for a translation service in sales. After they let me go (my heart really wasn't in it), I was unemployed for a long, long six months. I wrote to every single record and music company looking for a job. Somewhere at home I've got an envelope with seventy three rejection letters in it. I used to dread that moment when the post came, as I opened the envelope and hoped not to see the word "unfortunately" on the first line! Eventually I got a offered a job with Tumi Records in Bristol. I told them I had to speak to my current employers. I rang Tumi 30 seconds later and said "I can start tomorrow!

B&A: From the things you did in music, what have you brought with you into your current career?

MM: I've brought so much. How to treat people; how not to treat people. How to lead a team; how not to lead a team. Management, marketing and PR tasks. How to deal with the creative process. Learning how to project manage the making of an album, including art directing the cover - these are all transferable skills that go into creating a menu in a restaurant.

B&A: Most jobs are very different on the inside to how they look on the outside. How did being in the restaurant business differ from your external preconceptions?

MM: It's been a million times more enjoyable than I can ever imagine.

B&A: How long had you dreamed of doing this?

MM: I'd been planning the move for ten years.

B&A: Ten years? What took you so long to make the move?

MM: There were many reasons: the market wasn't ready for something Peruvian. I knew that and I felt that while I was tracking that. But I wasn't ready. I had safer options. I had to concentrate on taking care of my wife and raising a family, and I wasn't equipped in terms of leadership, so I learned and took my time. It's the same as my marriage: I was very methodical! Waiting is one of the assets anyone can have.

B&A: How do you know when to wait and when to act?

MM: You just have to feel it. I've never got it wrong so far - maybe on the small stuff, but never on the big stuff. I get dishes wrong all the time. I think "this dish is going to take London by storm" and that happens with just 3 out of 10.

B&A: Well that sounds like a music A&R process right there!

MM: That's it. That's exactly what it is!

MARIA McCLOY

Maria is a natural born accessories addict and can remember falling in love with the markets where she grew up as a child (Sudan, Nigeria, Mozambique and South Africa). Whilst working as a PR at VIMN Africa working on MTV Base, MTV, Nickelodeon, VH1 and BET, she came up with a branded African print clutch bag and her own line was born. Maria's line rapidly evolved and her men's and women's shoes garnered her more attention than ever, from Cosmopolitan, CNN Inside Africa and The Sunday Independent. Her passion for Africa and adornment continues to grow as she travels the continent for inspiration and new ideas.

MM: I've known a lot of artists who have died. I think I can name six, but there are definitely more. Actually no. Hang on it's more like 15. I'll send them all to you. People die a lot here. It reflects society. AIDS, car crashes, gun crime and the rest. Most of them die before they are 50. That's normal.

[They arrive on email after our conversation but here is the list: Brenda Fassie, Lebo Mathosa, Malaika, Mafikizolo Tebogo, Madingoane, Mawillies, Vuyo Mokoena, Sizwe ``Lollipop" Motaung and S'bu ``SB", Thanjekwayo, TK , Brown Dash , Miriam Makeba, Zombo, Thuli Thillies, Dr Mageu, Senyaka, Busi Mhlonga, Frank Leepa, Moses Molelekwa (a pianist Andrew Missingham produced and worked closely with), Moses Khumalo, Gito Baloi, Mizchief, Flabba, Lucky Dube.]

B&A: That's a large proportion of young creative people to pass away. What effect does this level of death have on a culture's creativity?

MM: Well it's interesting. Many of the post-apartheid 'hopeful' generation have died. But this last year has been a great year for music in South Africa. I started in the 90's and there are people in their 20's making those 90's sounds again and really influencing hip hop. So for the first time South African hip hop sounds South African and not American wannabe. It's like a more sophisticated version of

Kwaito (a South African version of house music using African samples and sounds). But of course, when people die it impacts. We don't have Lebo Mathosa any more. She was amazing. She was one of the super stars of the 90's and then she dies in a car crash. Not having her on the scene does have an impact because she was an amazing performer and she could have fed into the scene. But the industry is still thriving. Lots of new flavours and forms.

B&A: You've worn many hats in your career. Does your existing career make you think any less of your old one?

MM: I don't see myself separately in that way you know? It's all kind of linked. I started out with a media company that was about reflecting culture. We had a record label and our web magazine was a first and it was in that industry where I met everybody I needed to. Right now I'm primarily a publicist but I'm into lots of things in fashion, art and music and then I also make an accessories range too. Even when I was publishing I was selling vintage clothes and then in 2011, I started making things. So I don't really see that the old Maria ended. I still write sometimes. I could still work on a TV show. I still do publicity and then I have accessories. It works for me and I get a lot of attention because I am a publicist and at the same time I know famous people and they wear my stuff - so it's all very symbiotic.

B&A: Out of all the things that you do is there anything in particular that you learn the most from?

MM: Well I'm a baby in the fashion world. I'm giving my range a bash. I'm learning a lot about supplies and distribution. It's totally different to what I'm used to but in a way I do see so many parallels with music. It's just like releasing an album that no one knows about. I always say that music and fashion are the least glamorous industries because right now fashion is hard. I love learning it all. Like shipping, customs, international distribution and internet sales. Some of it links to what I used to do but some of it is totally new. It's a lot of dealing with people which is what I'm used to I guess. So I'm not only learning from the new stuff I'm also learning what I learnt doing my old stuff.

B&A: You ran the cutting edge online magazine in South Africa, Black Rage. What were your biggest learnings from that experience do you think?

MM: My thing with everything is to just do it. That is what I learnt from that time. There will never be a right time. Nowadays it's all about finding a sponsor before you do that kind of thing, but I would say just start. If we had waited for all the stuff you think you need when you start then we wouldn't have done it at all. We really learnt how to do things on very little budget. It's easy to do things on no budget until you hit about thirty two. Then you are like wait a minute, we're not making any money! Primarily what I learnt was financially-related. My current business would fall apart if I didn't have the financial backing and advice that I have. The reason we collapsed was that our main income came from our TV work and in South Africa there was only one source of money really and that was SABC. That subsidised everything. But then SABC collapsed and the entire TV industry collapsed in South Africa.

B&A: So what was the difference in learnings from your production company and your magazine?

MM: So much of what we did was groundbreaking but at the end of the day we just wanted to make media for people like us. The main learning was about financing, as I said. This is something creatives are struggling so much with today. I'm in the fashion scene and I go to fashion weeks where I know for a fact that so many people showing work can't afford to produce.

B&A: Is that because there isn't enough money to go around? Is it because the young creatives aren't great at communicating their ideas and so people don't see the value in them? What's the barrier?

MM: I think that firstly people don't know where to find money. A lot of times you are creative but you don't have a business mind. There needs to be more of a link between the business, corporate and the arts world. It's funny you know. So many people ask me just to send a few contacts to them. But I'm like hang on, that's my work! It's not like I can ask them to give me a free dental consultation! If it's art or culture people don't want to have to pay at the door. There is little respect for art and music as professions as a whole. That's what everybody says at these funerals - why did they die poor? Why is artistry not respected? Why do corporates deserve money but not artists? Why is creativity so often seen as a hobby?!

BdtA: So Maria, whoro do you look for inspirational innovation?

MM: As you guys know, the best innovation lives where you least expect. Urban culture is not the kind of thing that has patrons, or official support or attention. But it's the root of the most interesting stuff. A lot of fashion begins somewhere underground and grimy and then it hits the cat walks. To make my accessories I go to Zulu beadworkers in a traditional market which is just round the corner from where I sell my stuff in the hipster market. It's literally 5 mins away. But all the hipster middle class people would never venture 5 minutes off the normal route to find these kinds of places. They don't expect it. It's a traditional Zulu market where you can buy outfits and medicines and it's in what used to a horse stable. It's dingy. And that's where I make the shoes that will be in Elle or Grazia magazine.

I don't think the people that buy from me would have an idea of where this kind of creativity comes from. Nobody would expect a township, which is a place of oppression to produce so much music and creativity. Street style is the same. I really like seeing how a guy can put together second hand clothes that only cost 20 rand and make their outfit. This is style that comes from the hardest places to live. You see this kind of innovative stuff from those places. Conditions of oppression are not supposed to bring out music and art and creativity but they do. They really do.

draw your history

A GAME THAT OPENS UP <u>CONVERSATION</u> & <u>HONESTY</u>

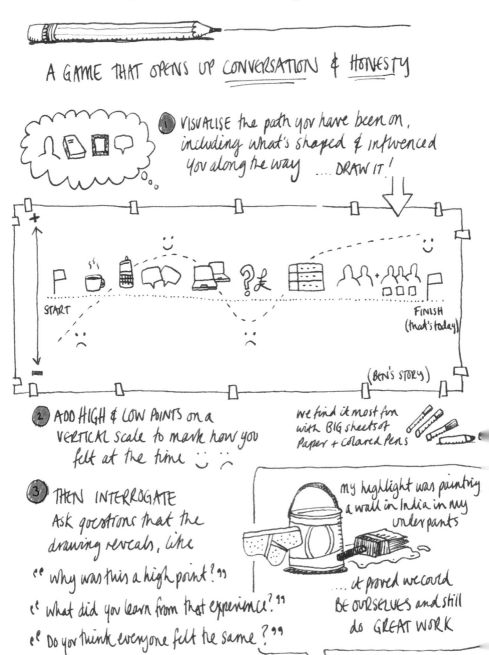

① VISUALISE the path you have been on, including what's shaped & influenced you along the way .... DRAW IT!

START

FINISH (that's today)

(BEN'S STORY)

② ADD HIGH & LOW POINTS on a VERTICAL scale to mark how you felt at the time ☺ ☹

we find it most fun with BIG sheets of paper + coloured pens

③ THEN INTERROGATE Ask questions that the drawing reveals, like

"why was this a high point?"

"what did you learn from that experience?"

"Do you think everyone felt the same?"

my highlight was painting a wall in India in my underpants

.... it proved we could BE OURSELVES and still do GREAT WORK

(ANDREW'S STORY)

UR GAME HERE ⟶

NOTES:

7. WHEN IN DOUBT CHOOSE

For years I've had a screensaver with just three words on it: "Make the decision".

The thing about decisions is there's always a decision following it (until you're dead, I guess), so you might as well crack on.

I learned this when I led an arts consultancy over a decade ago. We were producing a festival and the pdf run-outs of the flyer arrived in our project manager's inbox.

"Ooh, these are nice!" she said. "We've got two options, one in red, and one in green. Hmmm... the red or the green?"

A crowd of staff gradually gathered round her computer.

"Mmmm... the green's good."

"I prefer the red."

"Maybe we could ask them to redesign mixing the two?"

I sat stubbornly at my desk.

"What do you think, Andrew?" someone eventually asked.

"The red. Definitely."

"But you haven't even seen them" my project manager opined.

"I know, but let's make a decision and move on."

I very much doubt fewer tickets would have sold one way or other. And anyway, that's another thing - there are very few decisions which are irrevocably wrong (unless they lead to your death, I guess).

So with that considered, why is decisiveness such a rare commodity? Is it the plethora of choices? Is it politeness, or a desire not to offend? Is it the fear of getting it wrong and "failing", or perhaps fear of missing out on passed-over opportunities, by burning metaphorical bridges? (and on that subject, when we talked to Felix Barrett about bridge burning, his optimistic assessment was "even then, a bridge can always be rebuilt!") This chapter's provocation is a call to arms to be more decisive. Now get on and read it, or skip this chapter, or put the book down and do something else. Go on. Do it now!

FELIX BARRETT

Felix Barrett founded Punchdrunk after studying drama at Exeter University. Dissatisfied with conventional venues, he fell in love with site-specific theatre. Punchdrunk started a wave of immersive, experiential theatre that aims to erase the fourth wall as much as possible. From the start, Barrett and his team knew how to create interventions on a grand scale with minimal resources. They weren't the first people to do site-specific, far from it, but they were the first to be bold enough to think huge. Their New York show, Sleep No More, has been playing to sell-out crowds for over five years.

B&A: When you're working, there must be many matters to consider coming at you all the time. How important is it just to get on and get a decision, any decision, made?

FB: You have to make the decision. Even if it's wrong. I learned this as a director. When working with actors or designers or lighting designers, to keep everyone strong and loving it, you just need to say something and pick one way and move forward. And sometimes by picking, you know that it's wrong and have to go back five minutes later and change it, but either way it provides some clarity.

B&A: Have you ever left making a decision too long?

FB: In one instance, we took a decision to build a set with white houses, and when we lit it, we realised that the light bounced all around. We immediately realised that we'd made the wrong decision. We should have painted it black. But if you change it, there'll be a cost. The alternative is to live with it and find another way to solve the experiential conundrum.

A wrong decision's always able to be fixed if you have enough time. The times when it goes really wrong is when it comes to the end and you're having to make so many decisions and there's no time to fix anything and you're making decisions blind. There has to be a modicum of rationale to any decision you take. You can always make something better. It's never a disaster unless you've burned your bridge. And even then, arguably, bridges can be rebuilt.

B&A: What's the hardest decision you've ever had to take with Punchdrunk?

FB: To admit that we needed to grow up as a company and have a new structure. What made it difficult was because I fear change and it's easy to get stuck in your little patterns and systems. It's sometimes difficult to see a way out of that. The vision for the projects can be huge but you'll have a vision for a simple day to day life. Changing that can be intimidating but can be the most empowering thing you can do.

B&A: So you've learned the decision making skill in your core area, as a director, and you're battling to make this skill transferable into other areas of your life and work?

FB: Yeah, where you can now make a decision that can change your whole way of life but it's only a couple of steps beyond what you're used to and more comfortable with. As a people manager there are times when I have to take a decision that can change a person's life and this echoes one of your other provocations which can be as much of a sin as a positive: "be the person everyone wants on the tour bus". Clearly it's a positive but you can get distracted by it, trying to make everyone like you. You can lose people's respect. Sometimes people don't want a mate to have a drink with on the tour bus, they want someone who's going to tell them where the tour bus is going to.

B&A: Is it easier for you to reach a decision on your own or with others?

FB: With others. Every time. I need a foil. Someone to bounce ideas off. I think even the act of just talking an idea through can help.

B&A: That implies that it can be anyone, not just a special person who understands you more deeply.

FB: If it's always the same person, then that's a hindrance. Today I had to make a decision so I deliberately chose two people who knew nothing of the situation. One responded one way, one the other. From that it cemented what I thought. Before I couldn't see the wood for the trees but this process that led to "I agree with you, not you" gave me the confidence to own my answer. I've really learned that. Although I like the idea of creating in a cabin and coming out 12 hours later with a finished manuscript, I couldn't do it. I could never be a playwright. Every idea I've had has needed to be reflected off someone else. It has to bounce off someone. Maybe it's about self-doubt. In your internal dialogue about any decision, you can lose track of which side you really believe. As soon as you externalise it, it's out in the ether and you either agree or don't agree as you take one side or another of your split personality!

B&A: So how do you decide which creative work you take on?

FB: Actually, I think "creative work" is a misnomer. It's the love that's crucial. It's an instinctive response. If you love your work, if you say yes to yourself, it'll be completely fluid. If not, your head kicks in and you interrupt that flow. Then it's like a river that goes off course. You end up off the beaten track and lost in the wilds. Basically, If you're not happy, you're not going to create good work.

B&A: Where does that leave the notion that artists have to struggle?

FB: You still have to struggle but you struggle with what you love. You always struggle to get it out. I love all ideas at the beginning, but there comes a point when as they come close to being realised the more and more difficult they become and this can turn to hate. That's why you need to know you once loved it and will again. It's the birth process I guess, isn't it?

B&A: How do you maintain the memory of the love in that difficult moment?

FB: For me, love isn't a rational process: your body's responding, rather than your mind. If I can hold on to remembering that the project is initiated by my body, even though there are later more challenging stages where my mind is trying to implement, you have to go forward - so you switch off the "logical" mind.

B&A: Can you learn this, or is it an innate habit you have, and just have to practise?

FB: That's a really good question. It depends on the kind of mind you have. I find it difficult because I wear my heart on my sleeve. You can learn to love someone else's project just as much as your own, so I guess it's about belief in the idea as much as anything else. The idea has to speak to you and your own core values, or you have to believe that the idea speaks to your "target demographic" - the audience that you intend to be engaging with the realised idea. This makes it about empathy too. So it doesn't have to be your love, it can be the love of the people you're aiming at.

B&A: Is this something you've always done, or did you discover this way of approaching your work?

FB: I discovered it when I broke it. The first time I did something that I didn't love and it wasn't very good. If you don't love the idea, you'll take shortcuts. You'll want to be elsewhere and you won't care. It's like nurturing a plant. You want it to be beautiful but if you don't love it, you'll forget to water it and it'll just wither and die.

B&A: How do you inculcate this idea in your team? Do you look for this "loving" capacity before you recruit? Or do you teach and nurture it once they're there?

FB: All I know is that it has to be top down. The projects that have gone wrong are ones where I've thought, "I don't love it". This breeds dissent in the ranks and everything falls apart. It's my job to share the love and enthuse the team so they in turn love the work. I have to give them reason to love it. I want to see their eyes light up in the same way my heart does when it first arrives on an idea. The part I love about the process is that moment when I walk an audience through a new building - I did it last week when I walked people through a building in LA - and seeing their eyes light up and have them think "oh my gosh, this is going to be great".

priorities

A GAME TO PUT COMPETING IDEAS INTO A STRICT PRIORITY

(1) CHOSE A QUESTION that has MULTIPLE answers. EG "What do I need to do today?"

(2) WRITE 1 answer per card

(3) SET A QUESTION that has a SINGLE answer. EG "If I only did one job today, what would it be?"

(4) PUT 2 CARDS at random side by side & face up on the table

(5) ASK YOUR QUESTION, then pick 1 answer. Put the losing card to one side.

Which one is most important?

6 REPLACE the losing card & play step **5** again (until there are no more cards)

The remaining card is your winner & TOP PRIORITY

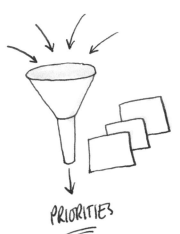

PRIORITIES

7 SHUFFLE the remaining deck & play again at least 3 times

The next round winner is your 2nd priority, the next 3rd, etc...

THIS can ONLY be played 1 on 1. If there's a group, they'll have to watch, listen & be <u>silent</u>

The game gives EVERY possible CHOICE an EQUAL amount of attention, which is why it's very hard to commit to.

DIFFICULTY RATING ✪ ✪✪ ✪✪

balloon juggling

A GAME TO FOCUS ON KEEPING THE MAIN THING THE MAIN THING

1 BLOW UP LOADS of balloons and get your group to stand in a circle around them

2 INSTRUCT the group they must try to keep **3** balloons in the air All the time....

... then toss them one balloon, followed by another & another & ....

3 BLOW a whistle every time a balloon hits the floor. It adds tension & further distraction

4 WATCH what happens. It usually descends into CHAOS as the group chase All the balloons.

5 LOOK OUT for when the group start ignoring distractions & tension and focus on achieving the TASK

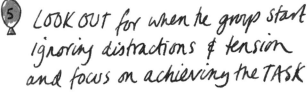

OUR GAME HERE

NOTES:

8. THE FURTHER THE THESIS FROM THE ANTITHESIS THE GREATER THE SYNTHESIS

Hegel's triangular logic of an idea (the thesis), an opposing idea (the antithesis) and the resulting answer when they come together (the synthesis) is one of the cornerstones of how we approach problem solving. Finding an opposing view that's far enough away from the original to make the answer exciting is our constant challenge.

Imagine if you were going to create a new kind of soap powder. You decided to mix Sudso Brand X with Sudso Brand Y to create New Sudso Brand Z. That would not only be extremely unexciting, it would also likely fail. The thesis (X) and antithesis (Y) just aren't far enough apart to create a synthesis that is different enough to be compelling. Now, mix Sudso Brand X with a wet Chihuahua dog, and throw the pooch into hot water with your smalls, well, then (animal cruelty aside) you'd have a whole new way of doing things that could lead to some really creative thinking.

To find new stuff, you've got to look in unexpected places. You've got to be prepared to be surprised, shocked even. This means that creativity is hardwired into diversity. Monocultures are biologically unhealthy for a reason. The provocation in this chapter dares you to look further, deeper and wider to uncover answers that are unexpected, answers that wilfully demand you explore new territory, and are all the more wonderful for that very reason.

DYLAN WILLIAMS

After graduating from the London School of Economics, Dylan joined BBH as a strategic planner and worked across the London and New York offices over ten years, most notably helping steer Levi's through the 'denim apocalypse' of the late 90's. He was quickly promoted to the board as its youngest director and shareholder. From BBH Dylan headed to acclaimed London creative agency Mother, where he became partner. In his ten year tenure, Mother was awarded both 'Campaign Agency of the Decade' and the prestigious Stephen King 'Best Global Strategy Agency' accolade. Campaign magazine also voted Dylan the industry's number one strategist. Dylan is currently the Global Chief Strategy and Innovation Officer at Publicis Worldwide. He is the co-founder of the Drugstore, a start up innovation and enterprise facility in East London, which fosters relationships between start ups and multinationals.

DW: I always have problems with Hegel's dialectic.

Most of the problems I've helped solve, or strategies I've helped create, sit in the sweet spot of tessellating areas of enquiry, and yes, this is a form of synthesis, but Hegel's dialectic - setting up an idea and its anti–idea - does tend to constrain enquiry into two dimensions. This way of thinking takes as read that you have a bookended spectrum and you find something in between.

For me, it is important to try more dimensions. Saying that the answer lies between thesis and antithesis just isn't dense or rich enough. But an augmented form of that dialectic, that adds at least one, ideally two, further axis, and allows one to think in, say, Euclidean Space, does describe how strategists like me go about trying to find solutions. When I look for answers on behalf of brands, using this richer range of dimensions, I look to find something that's relevant to the people, credible to brands, distinctive in the market, that positively contributes to culture and deploys media in the right way. If you've got all these five, you've usually got something that's going to work. The economist, Thomas Sowell, said "there are no solutions, only trade-offs". Maybe, but for me, the more inputs incorporated in pursuit of solution, the more we reduce its eventual opportunity cost.

B&A: I guess then, that one of the reasons that this dialectic has been so persistent and widely adopted is precisely because it's so easy. The nature of an "antithesis" is that it's held in the thesis. The opposite of black is white (in other words another colour, that has a lot in common with its counterpart). So it's two sides of the same idea.

DW: Yes. Definitely.

B&A: So how do you encourage people around you to find more diverse answers to their questions, step outside their comfort zone and explore?

DW: People must embrace serendipity. To hark back to Heisenberg's Principle of Indeterminism, you're going to affect that which you observe. You'll affect the outcome. So any conscious pursuit of an answer will affect the direction of enquiry and this will usually justify what you're looking to find justification for. That's not usually the path to finding something that's valid and true. A complaint often made about strategy is that it's autobiographical. To refer to one of your other provocations, you have to go to 'the world outside your manor', and find something outside your inherent experience if you are to find more objective answers. Embracing serendipity sounds flippant, but it's about increasing the probability of something random happening that might take your perspective in a new direction, or take you out of your deeply held beliefs. This can be done with simple things like travelling to work a different way every day and without coming over all "Dice Man", you just have to do all you can to embrace random shit.

B&A: So you speak to the third person you see that day, no matter who they are?

DW: Yes. Or you close your eyes and point to an item on the menu, and have that for your meal. Do that to choose a cocktail. Or pick a holiday destination. (I've not done this one). You just do all you can to debunk convention and get outside habitual behaviour.

B&A: And when you go outside your habitual behaviour, you most often find other people's habitual behaviour - sub-cultures, if you will. A few years ago I tried that by going trainspotting. I got a copy of Rail Monthly, a flask of tea and a ring-bound reporter's pad and headed to the end of the platform at Liverpool Street station. I wanted to understand what trainspotters were looking for. When I eventually asked the genuine trainspotter, who was standing at the end of the platform with me, he told me that he was looking for "unusual things". He said - "Take that rolling stock, that's non-sequential. How did it come to be linked together? And look at that locomotive. Its livery is Great Western, but this is the East Coast line. How did it get here? It must have had to change at Crewe."

DW: That's great! Because the presumption from the outside is that the reason people get off on looking at trains is because of some sort of love of order, but he was looking for the exact opposite!

B&A: Right, exactly.

DW: The reason I defaulted to going to work a different way, is because I always loved the Sundance Kid. Sundance couldn't shoot when he stood still. He said "I'm better when I move". And I think strategists are better when they move, because they're constantly exposed to new stimulus, that wasn't necessarily part of their conscious enquiry, but nevertheless contributes in some way to their processing. I don't take deskspace anywhere I work. I've found that if I do, it starts to restrict me. I just end up in obvious places. I'm not that good.

B&A: How does this square with your role at Publicis? There's you - no desk, no office - in a network of offices with desks in them which people put their name by, have a mascot on their computer and get very attached to! How do you inspire these folk to want to break out of this comfort blanket?

DW: Usually working environments are temples of ratification and endorsement: global people tend to have big maps in their offices; yoga studios have buddhas and incense; creative people have lots of copies of D&AD on their shelves! They're all symbols of the world view that they've embodied in their role. And side by side, these create a patchwork quilt of different cultures and that's great. But I think it's a lot more healthy for a thinker to bounce between the myriad temples of belief systems, rather than sitting in the one that serves to confirm conventional wisdom. To answer your question, it really does come down to things as simple as not spending too much time in environments that make you too comfortable. The more time we spend around different people, the more we are exposed to new variables and things that bounce against your preconceptions and move them into new places that we hadn't anticipated. To use your language, the most interesting provocations are the random ones that you don't see coming. The worst kind of problem solver is the desk-bound problem solver.

B&A: When you talk of breaking out of this patchwork quilt of security blankets, you're really talking about risk. Was there a time that led you to this way of thinking - where you embraced serendipity, and the life of risk that leads to?

DW: The creative economy as it currently stands in the UK doesn't embrace diversity. Most of the people in this room at D&AD are white, from affluent backgrounds, and highly educated in a narrow set of disciplines. But what initially encouraged me to break out and explore, was that I wanted to get out of a pretty boring and shit environment. The vast majority of the people on this planet want to do likewise. And yet, we only currently recruit and train people who don't have that ambition. They just want to stay within the cosy, closeted world that they grew up in. And our creative economy pretty much reflects this. It's a self-perpetuating, and incredibly conservative, world. We surround ourselves with a very, very narrow demographic, so the creative industries in Britain aren't that different to a tiny Amazonian tribe in the middle of the jungle, that's never exposed itself to the breadth of possibility and humanity! And much like that tribe, our world feels incredibly secure, but it's actually incredibly vulnerable because it's a singular monoculture that looks inward.

B&A: If you were to do one thing for the creative economy that would encourage it to become stronger by becoming more multicultural or polycultural, what would it be?

DW: I would encourage motion. I look at 650 people dying as they try to get from Africa to Europe on rickety leaking boats, and I look at all of the great innovations in history, and I conclude that what drives us all is motion. When people explore, that's when they're at their peak – when they're pushing beyond frontiers. Those poor people died in pursuit of something new and better. There's something inherently creative about migrants, because of what they are trying to do. And alongside physical migration, read intellectual migration, or creative migration: looking beyond what we understand to get somewhere we've never been before.

crazy love

A GAME TO UNLOCK YOUR ABILITY TO THINK LATERALLY

1 WRITE DOWN ON INDIVIDUAL CARDS ALL the things you _love_ about your chosen subject. PLACE them face down on the table

2 NOW WRITE DOWN ALL the things that drive you crazy about the subject. PLACE these cards face down on the other side of the table

3 PICK ONE FROM EACH PILE & use the thing you LOVE to solve the thing you HATE.

The cards provide such OPPOSITES that their CLASHING can be a key to help LATERAL thinking & SPARK new ideas

The city is VISUALLY EXCITING!

the streets ARE DIRTY

PAINTING STREET WASHERS

HOOVERING BILLBOARDS

OR

OR

UR GAME HERE

NOTES:

9. MORE DOES NOT EQUAL BETTER

Less does.

RICHARD
ALSTON

*After two years at Croydon Art School, Richard Alston CBE was one of the
first cohort of students trained at London School of Contemporary Dance
in 1968. He then choreographed for London Contemporary Dance Theatre
before forming the UK's first independent dance company, Strider, in 1972,
taking time to study at Merce Cunningham Dance Studio in New York.
Richard has created works for Rambert, Royal Danish Ballet, UK Royal
Ballet and the Michael Clark company. In 1994 Alston took up the post
of artistic director at The Place and formed The Richard Alston Dance
Company - since then he has made over 20 pieces for the company.
Alston is internationally recognised as a master of his craft.*

RA: I'm with you on 'more does not equal better'. I've worked in this
building (The Place) for 20 something years and we are crap at doing less!

The same pressure is true for me as a choreographer. People always ask
me - 'Why don't you do this or why don't you do that?' Even though my
company does a lot of different things, the truth is I am only going to do
the things that come and really 'zing' at me. I'm not going to do more just
because I can.

B&A: What you are touching on is that the 'less is more' thing being about
a manageability or purity of the original concept, right?

RA: Purity appeals to me more than manageability. It always amuses me
when people say 'Oh Richard you are still doing what you believe in...'
It's quite touching isn't it? I guess its true though that there are things I
love about dance which fewer and fewer people are getting to deal with.
So, that's where I feel it's really interesting. Here we are in the middle
of this big scuffle about training, but one of the reasons I'm here is that
people come and want to dance with Richard Alston and they want to do
something that is difficult. They come with that focus. If I turned around
and said 'look times have moved on, you don't need me any more' then
those young people would lose that. My relationship with the students in
this building is really important. A young guy came to me last week.

He wanted feedback about something and wanted to talk honestly about why I couldn't take him into the company. I was very clear and told him. When I'd finished, he jumped off the sofa and gave me a huge hug. It's so great when you can be straightforward. And you can be with young people. They get it. You can talk directly and they understand.

B&A: For the book the first interview we did was with Amelia-Belle, Andrew's daughter who is six and a half. We wanted to ask her what a game is all about because if anybody knows what a game is it's a six and a half year old.

RA: We once did a big teaching thing in Scotland and I've never forgotten this amazing moment. There was a rugby teacher who really really loved dance. He was the typical big burly rugby guy in the borders - where rugby is a big deal and there were no jobs so you were either a rugby player or you didn't do anything. He said, "We had a big meeting last term because we see that less young people are signing up for team games. We sat down and tried to work out why this was the case. And the kids said that they weren't really interested in these sorts of team games because they were all about what you do wrong. You see in football you are always offside, and there is always a lot of whistle blowing and red cards and yellow cards." Actually in our lives that's not very exciting is it? So in the school they taught the kids skills and then got the team to invent the game they wanted to play. They got them to make the rules. So they had ownership.

B&A: You've talked before about keeping the company a certain size. Is there anything in restriction that can be an impetus for creativity?

RA: When you make dance you are making it with people. What I don't like though is crowd control. I love working with individuals and so a group of ten is perfect for me because you can treat them as individuals but you can also make a group act together whilst not shouting through a megaphone. It's a very particular skill to manage big groups but I don't try to do it. I'm only interested in taking the three people down the front to one side who are going to be the most involved. For me it's about conversation and making real human contact.

I see people expanding and I have to admit that I have always admired the American / Russian choreographer George Balanchine, but I don't have the confidence with groups that he had. He came from a huge Russian tradition of dance and so even as a young man he had a huge knowledge - and that gave him the confidence to do big things. But I never went through a full formal dance training and performed on stage. I came from art college and so it was a given for me that my performers were better than me.

B&A: But at art college your tube of red colour is always going to be a better tube of red colour than you are going to be and the clay is always going to be better clay than you, so you can't compare directly, but as a choreographer, when you are working with the human form, you yourself are human and the canvas you paint on is with other human beings. This begs an unfortunate propensity to compare doesn't it?

RA: I think that is one of the reasons why I've chosen to work with music. Because music has always been so central to what I love. I couldn't do so many things but boy could I dance to music! I think all creative people get excited by what they are good at and what is natural to them.

I always say to audiences that when you start tapping your toe then that is where dance starts. That is what I want them to see. It's ancient. It's so old it's too old to be old fashioned. It's never going to go out of fashion. I had a very good friend who was in NYC when I was a student. She came to see my company when we went to the US for the first time and she hadn't seen my work since we were students. She bounced up at the end of the programme she said "Richard, it's something for everyone!" I've always loved that.

B&A: Have you never been frustrated by the limits of the human form as a canvas?

RA: No. Because I start from the human being. That's why I am not interested in what you see a lot of, which is choreographers exploring how to distort the human body. I don't want to damage humans I want to find out how expressive they can be whilst they still look like real human beings. I'm interested in what this person can do and whether they can do something different but I'm not interested in asking people to put their heads on their ankles whilst their foot is towards the ceiling. That seems gymnastic and inhuman. It turns the body into an object and I don't really want to do that. I'm definitely beginning to realise that I know more about my work than I used to. That's helpful. Although I now know I know some things (particularly about my own work) as opposed to the contention in your provocation. I still say to dancers that I don't know what I'm doing. I never tell them we are making a piece because I know what it is going to be.

ROBERT COHAN

Born in New York in 1925, Robert Cohan trained at the Martha Graham School, where he quickly moved to soloist and then performed throughout the world as a partner to Graham herself. He left in 1957 to start his own small group of dancers and started his long career as a choreographer. Robert Cohan's influence on the development of modern dance in Britain has been enormous. Having pioneered the teaching of contemporary dance in Britain, he laid the groundwork for the many of Britain's most successful contemporary dance companies. Robert Cohan, now in his 90th year, has been continually in demand as a director of choreographic courses, notably the 'International Course for Professional Choreographers and Composers' which he directed six times.

B&A: You are now in your tenth decade, which was the most fun?

RC: Aha! Probably when I became a professional dancer. So, decades two and three. I was discovering the world of dancing as a professional. It was like the movies. There used to be these great movies about musical shows going on the road in a Pullman. It was like that.

B&A: What do you consider as your greatest achievement?

RC: Living! I thought I would die very young because I burned the candle at both ends for years and so I can't believe it. People said, 'Congratulations you are 90.' I said 'I think it's an accident!'

B&A: It's easy to ask "what's different?", but what hasn't changed as you've grown older?

RC: Many things have changed but one thing is the same - my choreography - and it still works. That is fascinating. Why does that still work when I can't walk?! Matisse just went on working no matter what happened to him but with dance that it is harder. I find the process of ageing fascinating. I'd love to write about it but I don't think anybody young would read about it.

B&A: You'd be surprised! Although ageing is a bit of a taboo and a mystery.

RC: Well I was always interested in the growth of my body as a dancer. In the same way as I'm interested in the decline of the body. What goes first? Why does it go at all?!

B&A: Is there anything that the physical restriction of ageing opens up?

RC: Well the obvious thing that is gained is that you get irritated! Everything takes longer. Everything is harder. George Sanders, the actor, supposedly committed suicide saying "too many buttons to button and un-button!" and when you are my age and you want to button up a shirt you know what he is talking about. I recently lost my glasses. I think they are under the bed but there is no way I can look for them. It's something as simple as that. All of those things change your ability to function in the world - which is something you have worked hard at. I used to be very strong. Now I'm very weak. At the same time what you do learn is what is essential and what isn't.

B&A: Do you think that creativity is hardwired in us from day one or do you have to develop and nurture it over time?

RC: You have to work at creativity. You have to work hard at it. First you must recognise the concept that you are going to create and then you have to go through the question of what it means to be creative. For me, it's all about focus and work. You have to have an idea and a date. In dance, what I did meant I started with a date in the calendar. The date would be when a new work would have to be finished because the company was booked for then. So, that's my 'creative worry' - I've got to work myself to finish on that day. It's no good just letting it happen. You have to worry about it creatively. I have to question it constantly. Is it the right approach? Is it the right idea? Am I doing it right? I just have to keep worrying about it all the time by having it at the back of my mind constantly. If you want a style, you have to work at it to find out what it is. You don't have it before you start. You can't just make it up. If you do then you are going to copy somebody else, or it's not valuable because you are not producing it from yourself.

Many people try and eliminate this difficult process. They ask people like me, 'Is this my style?' and they want me to say yes or no. But I don't know the answer. A person's style will emerge without them knowing it and that will be their real style. The moment they try to copy it they will be stuck.

B&A: Let's talk a bit more about the 'worry point' and the performance moment. Is that deadline a restriction or a liberation of creativity?

RC: The deadline is not the end of it, but you have to be ready. You get ready by solving the many problems you face in making the dance. But you need the deadline to get it done.

B&A: So in creating dance work, there are many things you have to attend to. What are the things that you concentrate on and what do you normally neglect or leave until the last minute?

RC: I come from a stage background. Therefore I know where I am going to put the work. I know it's a stage. I know where the wings are, I know where the back is, I know where the front is. I give dancers direction on where to come from because I think that spatial concept is part of the creation. I don't think about the costumes but I do think a lot about the lighting.

B&A: You've lit a lot of your own work. Tell me about the relationship between dance and lighting and why that is significant to you.

RC: Because you create in a lit space but the stage is just black. So the lighting designer is the person who shows the audience what you have created. You have to collaborate with the lighting. Sometimes when people light my work they will show me my work in a new way - which is even more creative because you are not always conscious of what you have actually done.

B&A: I'm interested in whether you learning to light has fed into your choreographic process?

RC: Sure! There is a point in Siobhan Davis's dance where a man, an important figure, suddenly lifted his leg and stamped it on the stage and the dance changed from there. I suggested to her that the moment he stamps the entire floor should change colour radically. It was a stunning visual moment. It amplified his stamp. That was a tool I then put back into my own creativity so lighting for other people has enhanced my own work.

B&A: Technology must have changed considerably through your career. Has it really affected your processes or just enhanced the audience experience?

RC: If you can use technology to tell somebody something that affects them and they remember it better as a result then that's great but you start to ask the question of what is creativity. To me, creativity should enrich the daily life of yourself or other people. You are creative because it opens new ways of looking at things. It gives you more sense of yourself as a person and it enriches your intelligence, it enriches your emotional compassion and all those things that we think make a better person.

B&A: So there is a kind of instrumental or utilitarian aspect to creativity, which is about it needing to relate to real life as opposed to just being for artists?

RC: Absolutely. More than anything else everybody wants to leave their mark. Even people who don't aspire to much. They still want to leave their mark. In the process of leaving your mark you create something and you feel like you are leaving something in the world. A gardener feels he created the vegetables he grew, a sculptor feels the beauty of the last image she created. All artists can't help but do it. There was a woman in the village in France who decided she wanted to be a potter. She loved pottery. She found she had an amazing talent for it and she made the most stunning pots very quickly. She bloomed. She felt like a new person because she had discovered a hidden talent in herself. That is the satisfaction that creativity can give. She has found a place where she can leave her mark for the future.

how to make a computer out of a cereal box

When I was a kid, I learned how to make a programmable computer using nothing more than an old cereal packet and some handmade punch cards. As well as it being a fun craft project, it teaches the relationship between inputs and outputs, and teaches the basis of logic gates in a really tangible way.

Here's how to make one.

You'll need a cereal box, some thickish card (like the back of a sketchpad), around 10 pencils or skewers, sticky tape, masking tape and a supply of thinish card (say around 10 old Christmas or birthday cards). The tools you'll need will be scissors and a hole punch.

1. Take a large cereal box and cut off the flaps, so it's open at the top.
2. Cut a flap out of the front of the box, to around halfway up.
3. Push this flap to the back of the computer and stick the top of it to the inside of the back of the packet.
4. Cut a slit along the front of the hole left by the flap on the front of the box. Do the same along the back of the box at the same height.
5. Through the slits, fit a piece of stiffish card about as wide as the cereal box. That is the 'enter' bar.
6. Along the top edge of the box hole punch around 8-10 holes on the front and back. Make sure these holes line up with one another.
7. Push a pencil or skewer through each of the holes.
8. Below the holes, put a piece of masking tape or something that can be written on (and replaced).
9. Measuring from the 'enter' bar to just above the holes at the top of the computer, cut around 10 punch cards from card that are around as thick as the cereal box.
10. Using the pencils or skewers to mark the cards make holes in all the cards so the skewers can pass from the holes in the box and through them all.

You should now be ready to start!
The holes at the top of the punch cards are "zeros". They denote negative answers. Cutting into the hole, so it becomes a U-shaped slot (so the skewer no longer holds the card if the enter bar is removed) denotes positive answers (i.e. a "one").

Let's think of some questions. How about "things that fly?"
Dragonfly, Jumbo Jet, Butterfly, Arrow, Hot Air Balloon, Helicopter, Space Shuttle, Fairy Frisbee.

Write each answer on a separate card, and put into the top of the computer. This is the data set

Now write questions that will reveal different answers (These get written on the front of the box on the masking tape, one question per hole).

Is it an insect?
Dragonfly, Butterfly.

Can it kill you?
Jumbo Jet, Arrow, Hot air balloon, Helicopter, Space Shuttle.

Can it hover?
Dragonfly, Helicopter, Fairy.

Is it made of metal?
Jumbo Jet, Helicopter, Space Shuttle.

You get the idea...

The holes at the top of each card are opened into slots to wherever the respective answer is positive, and left closed as zeroes where the answer is negative.

Keep the first hole on the front of the box without a question. Removing this will be like a mouse click that will execute the programme, so the corresponding punchcard holes should always be a zero.

To run the programme, take the "enter" bar out of the computer. The cards are now being held only by the skewers which denote negative answers between the holes and slots. All skewers are removed except for the "click" skewer. To input a question, push a skewer into the hole corresponding to the question you want to ask. When the "click" skewer is removed, the cards which answer this question will be outputted through the chute.

Input: *Is it made of metal?* (and) *Can it hover?* Output: Helicopter

The point is, you don't need lots of stuff to make even complex ideas a reality. Don't wait to have all the resources, all the technology and all the money. Because it won't arrive. Make something, share it and learn from it. If you can show somebody something (no matter how crude) not only will you learn from their feedback, you'll also have a chance to get them excited. Then they in turn will be more likely to contribute some of the things you might need to develop it further. Have fun and stay away from computers that are sugar frosted and dipped in chocolate.

the helium tube

A CLEVER TRICK TO GET GROUPS THINKING & WORKING TOGETHER

① THE SET UP make a longer paper tube in advance:

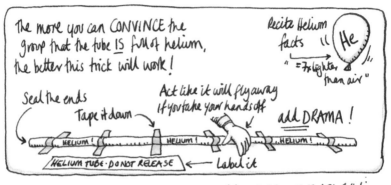

The more you can CONVINCE the group that the tube IS full of helium, the better this trick will work!

Recite Helium facts " He "
" = 7x lighter than air "

Seal the ends
Tape it down
Act like it will fly away if you take your hands off
add DRAMA!

... HELIUM! ... HELIUM! ... HELIUM! ...

HELIUM TUBE · DO NOT RELEASE ← Label it

.... they'll then believe it IS full of Helium

② THE HANDOVER
Get the group to form 2 lines facing each other & put their palms out. Carefully release the helium tube & lay it gently on the group's rows of hands. Make a big play of not letting it float away!

They must NOT touch the top of the tube!

③ INSTRUCT the group to LOWER the tube to the floor. This can only be done with team work & creativity. But the combined support of all the hands will lift the tube!

△ The natural tendency is to RAISE the tube

| The only way to bring it DOWN is to ▽ WORK TOGETHER

④ WATCH the group dynamics & strategies as they unfold

Taught to us by Margaret Macdonald at Wella Professionals

131

YOUR GAME HERE

NOTES:

10. THERE'S A BEST BEFORE DATE ON EVERY RIGHT ANSWER

Some of the best toys in the world are toys of construction. Think Lego, Meccano, even Play-Doh (maybe there's a pattern in the "oh!" exclamation at the end of all of these names that appealed to the copywriters and hints at the world of wonder these toys open up!) The irony is that all construction toys also have destruction built in. There's something deeply uncreative about building a Lego toy, just to sit it on a shelf to admire (and if you've ever known someone who does that, you'll have always known deep in your heart that they never really got the point). No, the play's in the circular pattern of construction, dismantling, learning and reconfiguring.

Sometimes you have to make a toy, just so you can break it.

We think that it's not only the breaking that liberates, it's also learning that your creative solution (the thing you've made) might be great today, but that doesn't mean it'll endure for all time. Solutions are a perishable commodity, that deteriorate over time, when context, opinion and even the weather changes.

To be creative, you need to create. And the best time to create is now, as time's clock never stops ticking. But you can't afford to get too attached to the things you've created. They'll have their day, and then their day will go. That even goes for occasions when you're trying to make something that'll endure (like a finished product, or an art work like a movie). You have to test, explore and let go, to find the right territory to build upon. The more you explore, the more likely you'll arrive at a work of quality. James Dyson famously made 1,562 prototypes before he arrived at his first production vacuum cleaner. That's not 1,562 wrong answers, that's a whole heap of right answers, if you're learning carefully enough.

This chapter's all about iteration and the creative learning that's inherent not only when you make something, pull it apart, learn from it and rebuild, but also when the evidence tells you need to leave your precious creation and explore another path.

VAIBHAV CHHABRA

A mechanical engineer by profession but a carpenter by passion, Vaibhav graduated from Boston University and then spent extensive time at EyeNetra, building innovative eye diagnostic devices for the mass consumer market in India. A few years ago, when he moved to Mumbai, Vaibhav co-founded Makers Asylum. He essentially coupled his degree with his passion to create the first community Makerspace in India.

B&A: To cut to the chase, while our Skype connection is good, why is making so important to you, Vaibhav?

VC: Firstly, I really believe in the iterative process of making. When you make something you have to first make it, then test it and then re-make it based on what you have learnt from testing it. So it's a constant journey of learning and testing. You can't make something that is perfect first time, it's just not possible. But more than that, I really love the collaborative nature of making. Collaboration is about different skills and people coming together to make things happen and the process of making is all about this. For example, often, artists know what to make, but not how to make it and engineers know how to make things but can't decide what to make. If they work together they can create something neither could on their own.

B&A: When we met last in Mumbai, you were telling us how making is a new thing in India. How can you create a new cultural habit when old ones are quite ingrained?

VC: Persistence. Persistence, persistence! (Oh, and a lot of self-motivation!) There are a lot of ups and downs in creating new habits. Much of your time spent can be demotivating and depressing: working alone or with a small group of people on something that nobody else seems to notice. The challenge is to stick at it long enough for people to start to see the thing you are trying to create. To get people to see the thing you are trying to create you also have to, to some extent, 'fake it to make it'. I never believed in that before, but now I do. You have to find ways to draw people in, to give them a taste of where you are headed, because it's hard for people to imagine it in the same way you do, especially if they are not as close to it as you are. At the same time, you have to be really positive. If your motivation drops, so does everybody else's. Finally, we also try to think about our Maker Asylum community of amateurs as professionals - we look at ways to create perceived value around them so people take it seriously and don't treat it just as a 'fun thing' but actually as something people are willing to pay for.

B&A: When we worked with you and Microsoft, it was great that you brought one of your 3D printers in. It really brought your idea to life. If you could make anything with a 3D printer what would you make?

VC: 3D printers can make a lot of cool stuff but actually I'm more of a fan of old school machines like lathes. 3D printers are great because they are repeatable. This makes the creation process easier because you can de-bug (like coding) rather than entirely re-starting. But fundamentally what 3D printers do is about repetition. I prefer spending time on the lathe machine, where you really craft something through thinking and making and thinking and making rather than sitting in front of the computer quickly repeating things.

B&A: So with that repeatability and iteration in mind, how hard do you think makers find it to completely throw out ideas and start again?

VC: To be honest in India it's hard. Makers get attached to ideas because they want to own them. Paper prototypes have really helped - because you can throw out ideas quickly but not many people are used to that method. Personally I know that I will probably make something hundreds of time before I finalise it and so I recommend that to people. I always try to explain that you have to enjoy the process of making and not just the final thing. Making is a journey, it's not about the end goal. Every time you build you learn more. Usually innovation does not come from a lightbulb moment, it comes from tinkering with something that already exists. It's the small modifications that lead to big changes like taking technology from one thing and putting it into something else and if you are making constantly then you are more likely to do this.

B&A: Are there any emerging technologies that are exciting you?

VC: I really like the innovation happening in the healthcare sector at the moment, like handheld medical devices that reduce any unnecessary need of doctors. This is exciting because it's about optimising time. Specialists that have spent thousands of hours training but are often found doing mundane jobs rather than focusing on their specialisms. If technology can take care of the mundane then specialists can specialise!

B&A: What do you recommend people do to get into the making habit?

VC: Start by fixing stuff! Just start picking up tools and making things at home like fixing a door or changing a light bulb. For me it all starts with the beautiful feeling of making something work for the first time, or work again if it was broken. Each time you do it you become more curious about how and why it has worked - and then you build from there. Most people here at the Asylum in Mumbai started by fixing their old toys. It's very simple to start but you have to start, you can't just talk about it!

B&A: One final question. Before our chat, we asked you to pick one of our 11 provocations for a creative business is there one that is closest to your heart?

VC: I think it would have to be "the more we know, the more we know we know fuck all". I like it because when you first read it, it's hard to understand. You have to think about it carefully to understand what it means. I like that because it's much like making: you have to think about what you are making as you are making it. At the same time, I also see this statement saying something else. This is that in a world where you are given so much advice and that you can 'know' lots of stuff, this overload makes you deviate from the thing you wanted to do. I found that with setting up Makers Asylum, so many people had so much advice to give me but I found the more I listened to it the more I ending up 'fucking up' on my own goal. My university lecturer always talked about it as survival bias. He said that people's advice is always based on their own survival bias, not yours. So you've got to take their advice very carefully and not just follow it all.

paper prototyping

A SUPER WAY TO EXPERIENCE AN IDEA AS QUICKLY AS POSSIBLE

① START !
The moment you DO something,
You start making PROGRESS.

WHAT ARE YOU WAITING FOR?
.JUST START!

❝ IN ORDER TO LEARN
YOU HAVE TO MAKE ❞

I MADE a hat to
protect me from the
weather....

IT HAD:
Insect barrier
Sun visor
Nose protector

② TEST
Experiencing the product yourself
puts you right in the shoes of
Your end user,
& gives you INSTANT
FEEDBACK

AS SOON as I put
my new hat on, I realised:
• Rain could get in at the top
• It needed 'hearing holes'
• It was too claustrophobic!

③ ITERATE
The great thing about PAPER
prototypes is that you can make
IMMEDIATE CHANGES which are CHEAP & QUICK!

④ SEE NUMBER ② ☺

OUR GAME HERE ⤴

empathy maps

A TOOL TO HELP YOU QUICKLY <u>UNDERSTAND</u> YOUR CUSTOMER
from our smart friends at XPLANE.com

1. BE SPECIFIC
   You have to REALLY understand
   your customer to design
   specifically for them.

An ACCURATE
snapshot of their
life

will help you get
inside THEIR HEAD
& understand their behaviours

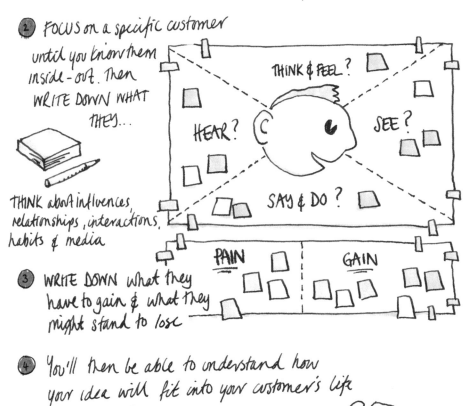

2. FOCUS on a specific customer
   until you know them
   inside - out. Then
   WRITE DOWN WHAT
   THEY...

THINK about influences,
relationships, interactions,
habits & media

THINK & FEEL?

HEAR?   SEE?

SAY & DO?

PAIN   GAIN

3. WRITE DOWN what they
   have to gain & what they
   might stand to lose

4. You'll then be able to understand how
   your idea will fit into your customer's life
      (if at all).

OUR GAME HERE ↱

144

on developing
a thinking toy

Developing new thinking for clients has often meant beavering away, then honing and polishing an idea until it shines with a high-gloss sheen, before sharing it with anyone else.

We don't believe in that. We prefer to take a prototyping approach, working closely in collaboration with our clients and the smartest, nicest people we know. We then co-create solutions and plans (this is the approach we've taken to solve the problem "how can we create a book in five days?")

But this works for ideas as well. A little while ago, we came up with a hunch about the relationship between content (stuff you create) and interface (the way you get at that content). It was just a hunch, so rather than sit and polish the idea on our own, before the big strategist-cum-magician theatrical reveal, we mocked it up and sent it round to friends inviting their comments. It was a 'thinking toy', so we sent it around to some friends who we thought might both have a point of view, and an interest in using the toy if it worked, and invited them to play with it and share what they thought.

Their answers were fascinating, not just in terms of what they added, but in terms of how they approached (or in some cases, didn't approach) the task. As a process for developing thinking, we try to do this lots. It's like the online equivalent of scrawling on a paper napkin in a restaurant.

Here are some of the comments, verbatim. Aside from their thoughts which really help to expose gaps in the model, and the edges of its potential use, one of the most surprising things is how many were flattered to have been included – and the 'smarter' they are the more self-effacing they were. This was reflected in the fact that several thought what they thought would have already have been covered by others.

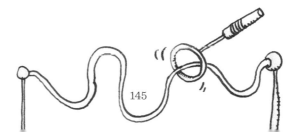

This exercise confirmed that a prototyping approach works as well for ideas as for real tangible things. In fact, the sooner you can bring in other people's inputs the better because your thinking will be informed by perspectives far beyond your own.

Have a play with the toy and let us know what you think too.

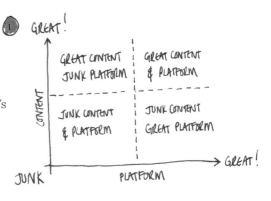

Matt Locke, Director of Storythings
I like this model, in particular because it illustrates the two pulls of content and interface. However, it doesn't really allow for a conversation about *context*, which for me is the most important factor in designing a new product these days.

Ruby Pseudo, Founder Ruby Pseudo
I like things being tricky, I like to have to tinker, in fact, I think flawed is rather beautiful, I mean, I'm a girl that writes in books, turns over pages, breaks the darn spine... I'm definitely not an interface girl, I'm a content girl.

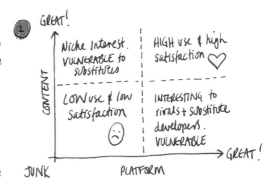

Aravind Baskaran, Lead Developer, Mowbly, India.
High on content, low on interface is stated as niche consumer interest. I think it even better fits enterprise B2B apps. The focus in such apps is more to solve a pain than to be attractive. In that sense such apps are also impervious to substitutes as they do not exist in the open market. Perhaps the quadrant does not consider enterprise B2B apps at all?

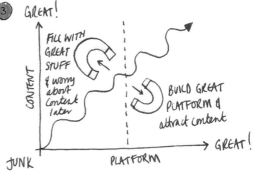

NOTES:

11. WE ARE NOT STORYTELLERS WE ARE SET BUILDERS

Storytelling seems to be so much the vogue (even default) motif of today's creatives the world over, it's verging on being a cliché. But you know what we really love at Ben&Andrew? Meeting someone like Giacomo Sbalchiero from Super Fred in Milan at the MakeMilano event we created for Microsoft, and setting the stage so he can tell his own story.

Super Fred is Giacomo's way of adding some missing human interaction to the digital age. His online portal allows you to donate a book to his virtual lending library, then go and meet the person who borrows it from you, face to face. Check it out at superfred.it. It's great, and Giacomo, naturally, tells his story better than we ever could.

Our journey to forming the structure that empowers people so they have the confidence to tell their own story, express themselves, learn, share and choose, is what's behind this chapter's provocation. Sometimes the structures are as simple as the pace that you work at, sometimes it's the language that you use, others might need a literal, physical stage to work upon (if you want a performer to perform, it seems nothing less than an audience will do). Above all this, the key seems to be creating a safe space. When people feel safe, things feel possible. When things feel possible, people open up to themselves and to others. With trusting, open people, empowered with a feeling of possibility, you can solve any problem in the world.

Our interviewee for this chapter, is Frantic Assembly's Scott Graham. He knows a thing or two about building sets to allow his actors to perform, tell stories, and create worlds of wonder for his audience, but in the Frantic Method, Scott's renowned method for theatrical education and personal development, he's a world authority on empowerment. As part of our interview he got Andrew and Tamika to walk on walls and fly round the room. It's a magical process - and once you've achieved that, the sky's the limit!

SCOTT GRAHAM

Scott Graham is the artistic director and founder of physical theatre company, Frantic Assembly. Frantic Assembly has built an enviable reputation as one of the most exciting companies in the country. The company has performed, created and collaborated in 30 different countries across the world. Their choreography can be seen in the West End and on Broadway in the hit theatre production, The Curious Incident of the Dog in the Night-Time. In addition to productions, Frantic Assembly also trains around 6000 participants in the Frantic Method every year through their Learn and Train programme.

SG: I think something that I've been able to see from the very start is how people's bodies move and how they can tell stories or express themselves.

B&A: Do you see what they can't see in themselves from an external perspective?

SG: Yeah, whether it's about what they give away in their body language or their potential for them to tell a story, or even achieve something. I think that the Frantic Method has empowerment very much at it's heart. I think it is part of the way we workshop an idea as well, that often meaning exists in why we're holding: it's not the sole responsibility of the actor or performer to possess that meaning when we explore it, we have to engage the audience as well. The audience is an intelligent and experienced being and they bring so much understanding to it: the actor can only possess a part of that.

B&A: That is absolutely fascinating. Basically, what you're saying, is that as a director, when you're working with actors, you too are working something out for a third party that's not there.

SG: Yes, it's a bit like the illusionist Derren Brown to be honest. He knows how clever his audience is, he knows how hard they work to find pattern and meaning. You have to empower your performer to realise they are not utterly responsible for inventing the universe from scratch, they are part of a process, a communion, they are coming together to ascertain meaning from situation. You empower them and you show them the world outside their manor first of all, and once they are in control of that they show the audience the world outside their manor.

It should be liberating for both.

B&A: How can you tell when someone is really learning something you're teaching them?

SG: It's when they do less. It's like treading water, there's control, their breathing is controlled, they are precise, doing exactly what they need to do to stay afloat and are doing enough to reassure everyone that they are not drowning. When actors and dancers really realise their own potential and the potential of their audience to understand, it becomes much more focused.

B&A: And you as a director or a choreographer, are there moments as an external eye where you have a hand in pointing out the choice that they're making, or do you leave it to them?

SG: It's about making them aware of the choice that they are making, then they can start to cut some of them out, or at least make clear choices. Once they know how contradictory some of those choices may be, they can start to approach it within an economy and that's empowering because, not only does it remind them how powerful they are to tell stories, it reminds them how powerful their audience are in reading those situations.

B&A: Now I get to ask my favourite question in the entire book: can you teach us how to walk on walls or fly?

SG: Yeah of course...

[Scott teaches Andrew how to walk on walls and Tamika how to fly. After a flight that's too short, they come back to land and talk again.]

B&A: What's the thing people normally want to talk about, or normally want to think about when you've taught them these amazing things?

SG: What they realise is it was simpler than what they were making it. People often jump or hide their weight: they apologise for their weight by hiding it and pulling away from the person lifting them, which just means they fall into the gap and it makes them really heavy. What you have to do is not apologise for the weight but push down; it's the two people working together that makes the person being lifted really light.

B&A: There's a certain sense of responsibility and seeing your own role within that activity.

SG: Yes. I think what also people like to talk about is the experience, they haven't seen the world from that angle for a very long time.

B&A: I was really taken by what you told us, you know, grown men who haven't been lifted from when they were children and that is something that is really powerful.

SG: It is very emotional. I found it to be very emotional because people get very emotional. One of the reasons I think lifting is very important is that is shows people they can do it, it breaks that subliminal message that it is only the ballerina who can be lifted and it is only the ballet dancer who can lift, that if you are not of that physique then you cannot do it.

B&A: Is that about permissions, you know what I mean? You have the permission to to be lifted...

SG: Yes, absolutely. I think so, because whenever I work with a group like that, and ask who wants to be lifted, when someone does shoot their hand up straight away and say"YES! Me. Yeah, yeah!" because the expectation is that you just want the skinny girl to go up. It's not about that, and I think that's another reason why it does affect people so emotionally. It's giving permission to take that role.

B&A: It's self-permission as well.

SG: Yeah definitely. It just really told me that the size of the denial, is bigger than I had ever imagined: more people than I thought were being denied, or denying themselves of that experience because they saw themselves as too weak, too old or too heavy... that's a worthy crusade isn't it!?

B&A: That's what is interesting because you really move seamlessly between the two parts of the Frantic Method, which on one side is talking about it as a dramatic technique for creating storytelling for the audience, then you talk about this other developmental tool for the people doing it, which is almost speaking to the audience members and telling them 'you can do this too'. That is what is really compelling and amazing about it to me.

B&A: How do you break creative blocks in others and in yourself?

SG: People find themselves trying to make work in a void: there are no reference points and the first marker they throw down in that void stains, sullies and is most often rubbish. I find constructing a process or game where it is safe to play becomes the first thing, and then so much of the creative process is about showing them the meaning of what they did even though they made it in a meaningless moment. You construct an environment where you show them that 'no, it could mean this' or 'it could mean that'.

In relation to breaking my own blockages that can inhibit my own creativity, I find it's most often about working out what's really important and then denying myself all the things I cling to and use as tropes, safe spaces or security blankets. Working in a team, I use the people around me to help guard against this. Once they know that this is what you want, and they're empowered to say, they can step in and tell me 'ah we've done this before, so we need fresh thinking' because we've all entered into that bargain.

the audience oath

In "Herd", a book by our esteemed foreword writer, Mark Earls, one of our favourite passages explores how to enlist people to interact directly to influence one another (for instance in an audience – where this peer-to-peer influence is so much stronger than anything we could transmit one-to-many from the stage).

It reminded me of something I saw years ago putting on a comedy festival when I was working at London's Institute of Contemporary Arts. I held some events in the bar where there was a lot of background noise. One comedian (if my memory serves me right, it was Adam Bloom) dealt expertly with the noise by enlisting the collective power of the audience to influence one another (and it's a trick Ben&Andrew still use). He just said into the mic:

"If you can hear me, say 'shhh...' "

The audience was given permission and empowered to take charge of the matter, and see their personal stake in helping the solution. The handful of people who were paying attention were enough to influence the rest of the crowd. They all shut up.

A little while ago, when I was talking to Kenneth Tharp, CEO of London's contemporary dance centre, the Place, he complained about the distraction of audience members using mobile phones to video performances, and how no appeals to the audience beforehand to stop this behaviour seemed to be working. He asked how he might find a more effective method of getting them to stop videoing and actually watch the performance.

Thinking of Mark Earls' insights and my memory of Adam Bloom's lesson at the ICA, I came up with "The Audience Oath". Feel free to use it at any performance (or even adapt it to use at a business meeting) where you want a little focus. It worked for Kenneth at The Place; it could well work for you.

The Audience Oath

(to be said to the audience before performance)

Please raise your right hand & repeat after me:

I do solemnly swear...
That for the sake of my enjoyment...
And the enjoyment of those around me...
I will turn to whoever is sitting next to me...
Should they use their mobile phone during
     the performance...
Be it to call, film, text, tweet, browse
     or status update...
And politely ask them to turn it off.

Amen

on "vertical video syndrome"

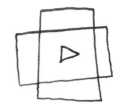

There's been a lot said about people who "accidentally" capture video on a mobile phone in portrait mode vertically. And none of it positive. Known as vertical video syndrome (or VVS), the august organ that is Urban Dictionary has this to say:

*"It is your duty to write, "You are not shooting it right, dummy!",
as a comment on any vertical video you encounter.*

*Origin: YouTube, where vertical videos have become a
major problem.*

A: I just watched a vertical video... It's sooo annoying!!!

B: Yes! The guy that filmed it certainly has VVS."

There's a very funny spoof public service announcement by Bento Box Entertainment's YouTube stars, Glove and Boots that captures the general sentiment well, stating that film screens, computers and TVs are all horizontal, so videos should be too.

Even the new version of Android gives you a subtle nudge to try and break the VVS habit.

Our question is, if the behaviour is so prevalent, why have so few people been curious enough to explore what's really going on?

After all, if, as Louis Sullivan stated, form follows function, then a mobile phone is tailor made for vertical video capture. The natural way you hold your phone for almost any other application (including calls) is vertical. Why should video be any different? Granted, a person with two working eyes placed where eyes normally are, have them arranged in landscape mode, but we think there's something else going on as well. If mobile is about personal connection, then

there's something in the name of each
photo aspect ratio that gives us a clue as
to the more natural modes for capture.
If "landscape" orientation is great for
scenery, for people, it's maybe better for crowds. By
contrast, "portrait" is great for individuals. And on a
mobile phone, where personal one-to-one communication
is part of the territory, and screen size is limited, maybe
shooting one person at a time, vertically, is better.
Moreover, people are made in portrait mode. It's the way
we've evolved.

And maybe history will
bear this out. As we write, a
current internet sensation
is versions of the rap
"Everybody Say Sausage".
The original, of a boy with
his friends at school, was

shot vertically (with a friend in the background also
capturing from behind - shooting vertically). Of course,
the subject is the kid leading the song. It would have been
a worse video if it was shot "correctly" in landscape (more
convenient for YouTube perhaps, but a poorer piece of
film). Even commercial video makers are getting the
vertical programme. The rapper Lupe Fiasco's new video
is in portrait orientation. I take my hat off to the A&R
who made the leap to realise that most of the potential
audience for the clip would be watching on their phone –
held vertically like a phone, not a game console.

Only by being curious, and to an extent, brave, can we see
and understand what's often in plain view, but ignored.

So too with VVS. It's time to stop fighting it and embracing
portrait mode as what your hand, and brain, naturally
want you to do.

Vertical video – it's the future!

walking on walls

* Ideally
SCOTT GRAHAM
Artistic Director
FRANTIC ASSEMBLY

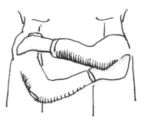

① YOU NEED YOUR BODY HOLDER to stand facing the wall. Put your hand nearest them on their shoulder nearest to you. They then place their hand under your armpit (sorry) almost grabbing your side

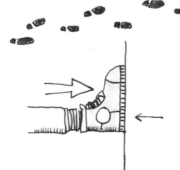

② GRAB ON TIGHT. Push off your body holder with your hand & place your foot high up on the wall. Your foot pusher pushes your foot INTO the wall

③ USE YOUR OTHER ARM for balance
& use your strength to bring your
other foot up onto the wall. Walk
up the wall until you're parallel
to the ground.

④ YOUR FOOT HOLDER now naturally
becomes your HIP HOLDER &
helps to keep you straight.
NB: It all happens very
QUICKLY!

⑤ REMEMBER you are walking
ALONG the wall now not up it.
REMAIN ACTIVE, engage your
core & keep pushing your feet
firmly IN TO the wall.

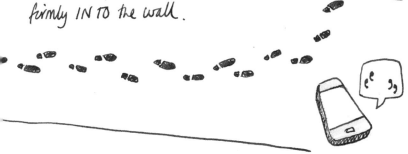

If you'd like to walk on walls, the BEST & SAFEST thing
you can do is call FRANTIC ASSEMBLY & get them to teach you.

www.franticassembly.co.uk

NOTES:

11 PROVOCATIONS

1. Listening takes all five senses

ROBERT: "At my age, you actually DO know somethi—

2. The more I know the more I know I know fuck all

3. There's a world outside your manor and I want you to see it

MELANIE: "It makes you a people pleaser, who forge your self

4. Be the person everyone wants on the tour bus

5. Have a Californian optimism and a wry British sense of humour

CHARLIE → But this can make you complacent

6. The work you do best is the work you love is the work you do best
.... as you stay in your comfort zone

7. When in doubt choose

DYLAN: This needs more dimensions,

8. The further the thesis from the antithesis the greater the synthesis
... a dialectic (with just 2) isn't enough

9. More does not equal better

LORD PUTTNAM: Some artefacts (like great films) endure.

10. There's a best before date on every right answer

11. We are not storytellers we are set builders

THE WHAT WHY AND HOW OF BEN & ANDREW

What is Ben&Andrew?

Ben&Andrew is a problem solving business. We use creativity to solve problems, be they business problems, cultural problems or social problems. In many ways we sit at the intersection between a creative agency and a management consultancy. Creative agencies generate and produce brilliant ideas that change the way that people think, feel and do things. But too often their ideas are 'campaign' oriented: they don't influence the essence of their client's business. Management consultancies are often asked to define and shape an entire businesses direction or activity, but too often they do not have the creative skills to find new and innovative solutions or directions.

We aim to bring the best of creative agencies and management consultancies together in a new kind of business that champions creativity and provocation as essential tools to achieve deep business, cultural and social impact.

Why did we create Ben&Andrew?

In essence, we aim to create a world of cultural, charitable, profitable enterprise.

Why these three ingredients?

165

All enterprises must be cultural because culture is what ignites peoples imagination so new possibilities are brought to life.

All enterprises must be charitable because today customers expect companies to offer more back to society than they take out.

All enterprise must be profitable because profit enables them to self-sustain and scale so good ideas are able to spread.

We believe that more cultural, charitable, profitable enterprises will lead to a world that's more authentic, legitimate and sustainable.

And that's really exciting. Because ultimately there is no alternative.

How do we work?

Our problem solving process that is built on a number of elements.

Firstly, our process centres on provocation. As you have read in this book, provocation is the tool we use to take our (and our client's) thinking to entirely new places. Provocation creates discussion, debate and dissonance. Provocation tests the edges of what one knows and where one is willing to go.

Secondly, our process is output agnostic. We don't pre-determine the output (because we don't have a business model that requires us to make a specific thing like a website, TV campaign, or app) which means that we can truly find the right answer to the problem at hand.

Thirdly, we work a problem's potential solution fast, we work it together and we work it over and over again. We don't believe in landing an answer through months of 'thinking' and lots of polishing. We like to get thinking out on the table and work closely with our clients to find the answers and develop them together. This means the answers we develop have been prototyped any number of times and are very much a product of our clients' work as well as ours. And that's why we've written this book in just five days. We hope you've enjoyed reading it as much as we've enjoyed making it, but of course, it's less a finished thing, and more the start of a conversation. If you want to share your thoughts or feedback, we'd love to hear from you.

All the best,

FURTHER READING

Here are some books we've read and have been inspired by over the last couple of years. We've chosen ones we believe will best help you to develop your problem solving, creativity, game-play and provocations. List is in reverse chronological order (most recently read, first).

The internet is not the answer - Andrew Keen
Who cooked Adam Smith's dinner? - Katrine Marçal
The Accidental Universe – Alan Lightman
Play – Stuart Brown
Information doesn't want to be free – Cory Doctorow
Gamestorming – Dave Gray (et al)
The Rudiments of Wisdom – Tim Hunkin
The Hard Thing About Hard Things – Ben Horowitz
Creativity Inc. – Ed Catmull
The Gift – Lewis Hyde
The People's Platform – Astra Taylor
The Universe Doesn't Give a Flying Fuck About You – Johnny Truant
Flow: The Psychology of Happiness – Mihaly Csikszentmihaly
Creativity – Mihaly Csikszentmihaly
10 Types of Innovation – Larry Keeley
The A to Z of Social Entrepreneurship – Liam Black
What Money Can't Buy: The Moral Limits of Markets – Michael Sandel
Finding Your Element – Ken Robinson
Herd – Mark Earls
The Better Angels of our Nature – Stephen Pinker
Prototyping – Todd Warfel
Juggad Innovation: Think Frugal, Be Flexible – Navi Radjou (et al.)
The War of Art – Steven Pressfield
The Upside of Irrationality – Daniel Ariely
Paid, Owned, Earned – Nick Burcher

Documentary Storytelling – Sheila Bernard
Small is Beautiful. A Study of Economics As If People Mattered –
E.F. Schumacher
Poor Economics – Esther Duflo and Abhijit Banerjee
The Bottom Billion. Why the Poorest Countries are Failing and
What Can Be Done – Paul Collier
Development Economics on Trial – Polly Hill
Goodvertising – Thomas Kolster
How Music Works – David Byrne
The Lean Startup: How Constant Innovation Creates Radically Successful
Businesses – Eric Ries
This is service design thinking – Marc Stickdorn, Jakob Schneider
Predictably Irrational: The Hidden Forces that Shape Our Decisions –
Dan Ariely
Economic Lives: How Culture Shapes the Economy – Viviana Zelizer
Governing the Commons – Elinor Ostrom
Adolescent brain development. Implications for behaviour –
Sidney Segalowitz & Michelle Jetha
Freakonomics: A Rogue Economist Explores the Hidden Side of Everything –
Steven Levitt, & Stephen Dubner
The Checklist Manifesto – Atul Gawande
Animal Spirits: How Human Psychology Drives the Economy, and
Why It Matters for Global Capitalism – Robert Shiller, George Akerlof
Thinking, Fast and Slow – Daniel Kahneman
Speed Mathematics Using the Vedic System – Vali Nasser
Priceless – William Poundstone
The Undercover Economist – Tim Harford
Africa: Altered States, Ordinary Miracles – Richard Dowden
The Logic of Life: The Undercover Economist – Tim Harford
The 7 Habits of Highly Effective People, Stephen Covey
A Pattern Language - Christopher Alexander
Fun Inc.: Why games are the 21st Century's most serious business –
Tom Chatfield
Reality is Broken - Jane McGonigal
Economics and Culture - David Throsby
Future Shock - Alvin Toffler
Cognitive Surplus: Creativity and Generosity in a Connected Age -
Clay Shirky
My indecision is final - Jake Eberts and Terry Ilott
Malcolm X – A life of Reinvention - Manning Marable
Le Freak - Nile Rodgers
ReWork: Change the Way You Work Forever –
Jason Fried, David Heinemeier Hansson

Drawing for the Artistically Undiscovered (Klutz) – Quentin Blake, John Cassidy
The Design of Everyday Things – Don Norman
Business Model Generation: A Handbook for Visionaries, Game Changers,
and Challengers – Alexander Osterwalder, Yves Pigneur
Where Good Ideas Come From: The Natural History of Innovation – Steven Johnson
Everything Bad is Good for You: How Popular Culture is Making Us Smarter –
Steven Johnson
Backroom Boys: The Secret Return of the British Boffin – Francis Spufford
The Adult Learner: The Definitive Classic in Adult Education and Human Resource
Development – Malcolm S. Knowles Ph.D., et al
Out of Our Minds: Learning to be Creative – Ken Robinson
How To Be A Domestic Goddess: Baking and the Art of Comfort Cooking –
Nigella Lawson
Your Memory: How It Works and How to Improve It – Kenneth L. Higbee, Ph.D.
Competitive Strategy – Michael Porter
Innovation & Entrepreneurship – Peter Drucker
Lateral Thinking: A Textbook of Creativity – Edward de Bono
Six Thinking Hats – Edward de Bono
Made to Stick: Why Some Ideas Take Hold and Others Come Unstuck –
Dan Heath, Chip Heath
Families and how to survive them – Dr Robin Skynner, John Cleese
They kill you in the end – Hal Missingham
The Spirit Level: Why More Equal Societies Almost Always Do Better –
Richard Wilkinson, Kate Pickett
Communication Power – Manuel Castells
Me and My Web Shadow – Antony Mayfield
Whoops!: Why Everyone Owes Everyone and No One Can Pay – John Lanchester

If you'd like Ben&Andrew to help you tell
your story in a book in five days, then get in touch.
We'd love to help, and now we know how.

Just cut out and fill in this form, and send it to:

Ben&Andrew
c/o Publicis
82 Baker Street
London
W1U 6AE

or email us at:

projects@benandandrew.com

Your name

Your organisation

Your address

Your email

What's the story you want us to help you tell?